Gay Hendricks holds a Ph.D. in counseling psychology from Stanford University and is a professor at the University of Colorado in Colorado Springs. He gives workshops and lectures to thousands of educators and mental-health professionals annually, and he is the author of ten other centering books. These include *The Family Centering Book, How to Love Every Minute of Your Life*, and *The Moving Center*, the last written with **Kathlyn T. Hendricks,** Ph.D., California Institute of Transpersonal Psychology. Kathlyn is a consultant in movement education, a teacher, and a psychotherapist whose special interest is the psychology of the body.

Gay Hendricks
&
Kathlyn Hendricks

CENTERING
AND THE ART
OF INTIMACY

PRENTICE HALL PRESS

New York   London   Toronto   Sydney   Tokyo

For my parents, Priscilla and Robert Swift.

KATHLYN HENDRICKS

For Katie

GAY HENDRICKS

Published in 1987 by Prentice Hall Press
A Division of Simon & Schuster, Inc.
Gulf + Western Building
One Gulf + Western Plaza
New York, NY 10023

Originally published by Prentice-Hall, Inc.

PRENTICE HALL PRESS is a trademark of Simon & Schuster, Inc.

Library of Congress Cataloging-in-Publication Data

Hendricks, Gay.
Centering and the art of intimacy.

Includes index.
1. Intimacy (Psychology)   2. Love   3. Mind
and body.   I. Hendricks, Kathlyn.   II. Title.
BF575.15H46   1985   158'.25   84-18288
ISBN 0-13-122268-6
ISBN 0-13-122250-3 (pbk.)

Manufactured in the United States of America
10   9   8   7

Contents

Prologue

Love is the best thing human beings do. Love is our glory, and it is also a power. Love is so powerful that even a little of it can heal and transform our lives permanently. We may go to the ends of the earth to find love or to escape it.

What human beings most deeply want is a total, permanent experience of love. Beneath all the strivings for recognition, power, money, and things, what we really want is love.

But what keeps us from feeling it? Why is it that what we most deeply want is also so hard to get and keep? The reason is this: The power of love clears out anything in its path, and we deal with what comes up either in a way that lets more love in or in a way that shuts it out. For example, a man has been rejected in a past relationship. Along comes a new love. Part of him rejoices (love is what he most deeply wants), and part of him fears (because love is associated in his mind and emotions with rejection). Because there is part of him that seeks permanent, total love, his old harbored feelings of hurt and rejection must be cleared up. The experience of being loved by the new woman will bring these feelings to the surface. But how will he deal with them? Will he project them onto the new woman, expecting her to reject him? Will he set it up so she actually does reject him? Or will he see his old feelings for what they are— a flurry of old pains that are being cleansed and released by the power of his new lover's positive energy? Above all, will he handle the situation in ways that move him to a higher level of giving and receiving love, or will he perpetuate the old pattern?

There are myriad ways of shutting out love. There are only a few secrets of letting more love in. However, these few secrets are so powerful that we really do not need more. All we need to do is learn what they are and how to use them properly. That is what this book is about.

We have explored the problems in relationships in several ways. First, our own personal experiences in love and relationships have been the major proving grounds for the ideas and techniques in the book. We have come to a loving and creative relationship with each other through the ideas we discuss in the following chapters. In addition, we have a combined total of more than twenty-five years' experience in working with people in psychotherapy; our clients and workshop participants have been a broader proving ground on which to test and refine these techniques. Too, we are familiar with the research literature in both psychotherapy and relationship therapy because both of us have been working as teachers of therapists for the past decade.

Our own relationship is the most important element of growth and learning in both our lives. Although we may refer to the research literature and to our clients' experiences from time to time, we can guarantee you that as a couple we have personally experienced and found successful all the ideas and techniques in the book.

Our goal in the book is to study the process of developing and keeping a close relationship in highly personal detail. We want to listen to the heartbeat of intimacy, to explore what it actually feels like to overcome the barriers to having ecstatic, creative relationships with other people. We know it can be done, and we want to see more of it in the world.

In our view, the opportunities in relationships for psychological and spiritual growth are infinite and the rewards boundless. What could be better than the clear experience of love and having persons with whom to celebrate it? Let us open the book of secrets together and discover the surprises that await us.

one
The Secret

We come into relationships with high hopes and a history. The history consists of personality problems stemming from past experiences. The love and positive energy that are generated between two people bring the problems up to the surface.

Here are some examples of personality problems:

- I feel unlovable deep inside.
- I can't stand being criticized.
- I get moody and depressed for unexplainable reasons.
- I feel explosive rage.
- I want people to take care of me.

An odd paradox emerges. Problems like these are often thought to occur because of a lack of love. Perhaps this is true back in childhood when the problems are first set in place. But in our present lives it is the experience of being loved that brings the problems to the surface. Love heals, and the healing process first has to bring the problems up into the light. When problems emerge, we often do not know how to deal with them, so we retreat from the other person and blame the problems on a lack of love in the relationship.

If you do not think you are worthy of positive attention and love, you will likely feel uncomfortable when you get some. Try an experiment some time that we have done with hundreds of people in our relationship workshops. It is designed to help you explore any barriers you have to receiving positive energy fully.

Get a friend or mate to stand facing you. Have that person look you squarely in the eye and say sincerely to you every ten seconds or so, "You are magnificent." We are all magnificent, though we might not believe it, so the statement is strictly true. Have the person continue doing this for two or three minutes. During each pause, notice what happens in your mind and body. Some typical mind responses are:

- The thought "No, I'm not."
- The mind wanders.
- Racing thoughts.
- Blanking out.

Some typical body responses are:

- Losing eye contact.
- Feeling tension in the body.
- Feeling the urge to turn away.
- Emotions welling up, such as fear and sadness.

The point of this experiment is that nearly all of us have resistance to receiving positive energy. Every one of us can benefit from learning the ways we block it. If you find, for example, that you deflect positive energy by changing the subject or making a joke, you can keep an eye on this pattern in future situations. We will have more to say about this subject in a future chapter devoted to the various ways humans deflect positive energy.

A close relationship is like a cosmic searchlight that seeks out the absolute best and the absolute worst in us. When one person connects closely with another, the energies of the two people are combined and enhanced, creating the potential for the relationship to climb to new heights or to fly apart. The reason for this paradox is that a close relationship challenges two major fears that human beings carry with them: the fear of getting close and the fear of being alone.

Ideally, we would have the capacity for comfortably being very close to other people and comfortably being independent. In fact, few of us are completely at home with ourselves and others without some significant work on ourselves.

The problem in getting close is that in the past we have experienced shocks, hurts, and irritations in close relationships. These problems often go back to childhood. Take, for example, the situation of a young girl who likes to hug and be close to her father, who happens to smoke cigars that irritate her sensitive breathing apparatus. She reacts by sneezing, a perfectly normal response. Her mind gets three things tied together: closeness, cigar smoke, sneezing. Later in life she snuggles up to her husband, who doesn't even smoke, and she sneezes.

The mind works this way for good reason. It has to take snapshots of things that hurt you. You put your hand on a stove and get a burn. The mind has to come up with a way of keeping that event from happening again. So it shoots a picture of the whole scene. If at the time you burned your hand you also happened to be chewing your first mouthful of licorice, you might find that later in life you don't care much for licorice.

Unfortunately for us, the mind often overgeneralizes. Ideally, if we get close to Dad and he sexually molests us, we will simply stop getting close to Dad. But the young and impressionable mind goes one or two steps further and thinks:

- "Don't get close to men."
- "Beware of sexual feelings."
- "Tense up around men—you're likely to be violated."

So, we have the following problem to contend with: We have gotten close, we have had an unpleasant experience of some sort, and the mind has taken a snapshot of the general situation. What happens next is truly extraordinary.

Part of us wants to avoid further situations that are anything like the original one in which we were hurt. Another part of us must seek out similar situations, though, in a drive to clear up the painful feelings and be free of them. In addition, we seek out similar situations because there may be something we are looking for that we got only in the original situation. For example, we may have gotten approval and positive energy from Dad at the same time he was molesting us.

5

Part of us is wary of getting close, and part of us will never be satisfied until we experience total closeness. We will not rest until we are free of the burden of the past and in a relationship where the present is vibrant and loving. That is why we return time and again to the arena of close relationships.

Earlier we mentioned the fear of being separate. Ideally, we would feel self-sufficient and totally at home with ourselves as separate beings. We would at the same time be able to experience total closeness with others. The two urges, one toward union and the other toward independence, would both be fulfilled and would not be in conflict.

In fact, we often fear true independence as much as we fear closeness. Imagine the predicament the infant is in. The child gets close to its mother for survival. In the process of feeding and being held, the child becomes one with the mother, naturally letting go into the fullness and warmth. But as the child grows, it also must establish a firm sense of its own identity. The child must learn to explore the world, to make decisions, eventually to be fully independent. In both the getting-close phase of infancy and the later phase of becoming independent, there are many things that can interrupt and prevent the successful establishment of closeness and independence. For example, a man in his early fifties sought counseling because he had never been able to establish a close relationship with a woman. A pleasant, attractive professional, he had no apparent defects that would prevent him from attaining this goal. Upon exploring his early childhood, though, it turned out that his mother had been stricken with tuberculosis when he was born, and he had been prevented from being with her throughout his first year of life. He was mothered by an aunt during this time. Then his mother decided to leave the area to find a new life. She left him with the aunt, who later adopted him. This is one example, perhaps an extreme one, of the type of event that can interrupt the getting-close phase of childhood.

In the becoming-independent stage, any number of troublesome events can happen that keep us from being at home with ourselves in the world. For example, a boy developed rheumatic fever just as his stage of independence was beginning. He spent nearly his entire third year of life in bed. Later, in adult life, he seldom liked to go outdoors, and he had never developed close relationships with men or women, fearing that they might limit his freedom.

We can really never know if early events like these are the sole cause of subsequent life problems, nor can we prevent the odd happenstances of life from occurring. What we can always do, though, is notice our areas of limitation and move to understand and correct them.

The path for us as successful humans lies in learning how to become close to others so we are completely at home with union, and in becoming fully independent so we are at home with ourselves. The limitations caused by patterns from the past often prevent us from doing either. When we have the opportunity to get close, we may start an argument or find some ways of making the other person wrong. When we have the opportunity to establish greater independence, we may have an accident or get sick, forcing us back into a dependency relationship with someone.

Some examples from the authors' personal acquaintance are:

- The night before starting her first real job, a woman accuses her husband of having an affair (nonexistent, it later turns out). He storms out, thinking she's lost her mind. She doesn't show up for the job because of the domestic turmoil. For economic reasons they are forced back into a wary partnership rather soon, but it takes a year of wrangling before it becomes clear that she manufactured the whole event out of fear of independence.

- Another couple has a pattern of having major fights at the beginning of extended times together, such as long weekends and vacations. Although they eventually recognize that the fights come out of their fears of getting close, it takes a great deal of work to break the pattern.

- A man about to leave on a trial separation strains his back and has to spend a week in bed tended by his furious wife.

Most of our problems in relationship can be viewed as resistances to getting closer or getting more independent. We want these things so much, and yet we have so many blocks to experiencing them fully. What can we do?

First, let's accept that it is our personal resistance to love and positive attention that is at the heart of the problem. This notion is a tough one to accept, particularly if you have had a great many painful experiences in life. But this awareness keeps us from the deadly trap of thinking that it is the world or other people that are to blame for our relationship problems. Second, we need to develop some techniques for spotting and dealing with the old patterns when they arise. Subsequent chapters will elaborate on various ways of doing this.

Third, we must build new channels in ourselves for experiencing and accepting positive energy. We must learn how to let love in, feel it, let it polish our inner bodies, and appreciate people for giving it to us. We must become adept at giving positive energy to others. At first it can be awkward, like speaking a new language. Simply to say, "I like you" with no strings attached can be a real challenge if we are not used to speaking the language of positive energy.

Fourth, we must learn to let it be all right for ourselves and our partners to go through cycles of getting close and getting more independent. This is a tough one, because our initial tendency is often to experience fear when we get either closer or more separate. A relationship has to be large enough to hold both persons' fluctuations of getting closer and getting more independent.

With courage, kindness, and practice, all these things and many more can be accomplished. It does take practice, though, because knowing all these things in the mind does not convince the heart and the belly that they are so. Listen to an experience of the authors', recollected by Gay:

> We were taking a walk around the neighborhood one summer night. The air was especially sweet and clear. Kathlyn looked over at me and said, "You are really gorgeous." I felt my head go light; my whole body felt polished inside. It was such a strong "hit" of positive energy that I could barely stay in my body. I had the urge to change the subject, but instead I stayed with the feelings. In a moment I thanked her, and we continued walking. I noticed that the front of my body felt cleansed, light, and open. My back felt a lot of energy in it, as if it could become tense very quickly if I did not do something with the energy. So I put my hands on Kathlyn's shoulders and directed to her all the energy I felt in my back. "That feels great," she said. Then, I asked Kathlyn to tell my back that it was gorgeous, too. She put her back up against mine, breathed deeply, and communicated the message to my back. Then I felt balanced, both front and back feeling light and free. Along the rest of the walk we thought of several ideas we wanted to include in this book and some of the other projects we were working on.

This incident illustrates several important notions about relationships. First, even though you know all the ideas in the book, it still takes practice to let yourself experience positive energy completely. Second, a clear, direct hit of positive energy has a powerful effect on the body. It cleanses and purifies, and also stirs up any resistance that the recipient harbors. Third, the recipient feels energized, and the energy must be passed along to stay in balance. Fourth, the giving and receiving of positive energy is an enhancer of creativity. It is one of the nutrients that nurtures a creative relationship.

With an understanding now of the basic issues, let's study the process of getting close in greater detail.

two
How to Get Close

Human beings have a deep urge to get close to one another. Yet problems come up when we do get close that often make us regret we ever had the urge. Let's see if we can find our way through this puzzling maze so we can have the closeness without the problems.

We like getting close for several reasons. For one, it feels very good to get into union with another person so deeply that we lose our sense of self. There is a part of us, some call it the ego, that has carefully established a sense of I-ness. We very much need the security of having a sense of who "I" am. Yet we also thrive on letting go of that I-ness now and then to become fully unified with another person or the universe itself. When you are making ecstatic, passionate love with another person, you probably do not want anything, not even a sense of I-ness, to keep you from full abandonment to the sensations. So the ego comes with a paradox attached: You've got to have it, and you've got to get beyond it.

We feel very good when we mix and mingle our molecules with another person's. For millions of years of evolution one organism has been mingling with another organism to make something new. So deep in each one of us is an urge to cast our dancing atoms into a tango with someone else's. We love to play, and the more interesting games require a partner.

Because of several quirky aspects, these games can sometimes sting. One thing that can happen is that we open up, lose our sense of self, mingle our molecules, then get badly hurt. Another thing that can happen is that we can open up, then pull back in alarm when we see what is coming up from within us or the other person. Perhaps you have seen those little metal animals that have magnets in their bottoms. If you set them on a table back to back, they will spin each other around so they are facing each other. In human relationships a similar process takes place. We back into a new relationship with our minds still on past events. Then the magnetic attraction begins to spin us around so we can deal with the present face-to-face. At this point we often engage in massive resistance. The force of the other person's positive attention is pulling us in one direction; the force of our past conditioning is pulling us in the other.

The stress of these conflicting forces causes us to contract and, in effect, to go unconscious. Going unconscious does not mean simply blanking out, though that may occur. It means that we abandon our conscious intentions and begin to run on automatic. Up come our conditioned patterns from the past. If you have been criticized a lot in past close relationships, for example, you may get close to someone in the present only to find yourself pulling back out of fear of closeness.

COMMON WAYS OF PULLING BACK
FROM CLOSENESS

Here is our situation. We have begun to feel close to another person. The increased love and positive energy have stirred up our fears of getting close, and we have begun to engage in actions that will make either us or our partner pull back, thus lessening the fear. What are some of the actions that we typically take to pull back?

Going Numb

One common way of stopping closeness is to cut off sensation. You are in the midst of an intense sensual experience with your partner, for example, when suddenly you lose all feeling. Where did it go?

To use another example, you subconsciously feel very angry at your partner but do not let yourself feel it or talk about it. Later, perhaps in bed, you find that you have less feeling toward your partner. We cut off sensation in our bodies in some common ways. One way is to stop breathing fully, which shuts down our capacity to experience and respond fully. We simply are lacking the fuel that full breathing supplies. Another way is to develop tension, pain, or loss of sensation in muscles. Some of the muscles that are most susceptible are those that are involved in emotional expression: reaching out, pushing away, standing up for ourselves. A third way of going numb is to remove attention from the present and go to an interior fantasy world, perhaps constructing a grocery list or getting rescued by a favorite movie star.

Going numb, then, is one thing that can happen when we go unconscious. It is a way the unconscious has of removing us from a situation that we fear for one reason or another.

Making Wrong

When our fear of closeness is operating, we are very likely to find fault with our partners, to make them wrong for something they are doing or not doing. If we can transfer blame to them, we unconsciously think, then we can escape for a little while longer the burdensome responsibility of inquiring more deeply into ourselves. One nonverbal sign of making wrong is an increase in territoriality. Suddenly it becomes important to know what's ours and what's our partner's. We may feel intruded upon, irritable because they've left dishes in the sink again, conscious of our property and our space. Retreating and glowering is one option when we are making wrong; another approach is to brandish a nonverbal sword of grimaces, sighs, sneers, clucks, flounces, significant glares, and other indirect signals of disapproval.

To complicate matters, it is when our fear is running most strongly that it seems most clear to us that it actually is the other person's fault. Psychologists call this *projection*. The word is apt if you think of a movie projector as an example. If you were in the projector's place, with all those exciting pictures flickering on the other side of the room, you might find it hard to believe that you were the source of the pictures. Projection is a major problem in relationships; Chapter 8 will discuss projection in detail.

Running an Old Movie

Getting close to another person involves going out of control. Even if losing control is ultimately fun, it can be scary at first. So when the plot of our life begins to speed up and go along unfamiliar lines, we often dial up a more familiar script. Even if the old plot has not worked very well, at least it is predictable, less scary and easier to control. There is part of the mind that likes to do things the same old way, even if that way has not brought much happiness to us. At least it has kept us alive, and under stress the mind often dials up the programs that have been associated with survival.

In forming close relationships a major task is being conscious of the dramas we create based on our old scripts. A role will always feel flatter and less alive than genuine expression. If we look closely, roles have a familiar cast, a sense of repetition, and a deadening feeling (because we've seen it all before). Our partners recognize, usually unconsciously, when we are playing our old movies; they summon up a matching role for fear of disrupting the familiar pattern of the relationship. Chapter 7, on nonverbal aspects of relationships, will explore this problem in detail.

Power Struggles

Another way of avoiding closeness is by engaging in power struggles. Power struggles are characterized by such issues as:

- Who gets to be right?
- Who has to be wrong?
- Whose problem is this?
- What process are we going to use to solve problems?
- Who has the power to end the relationship?

Most of us have unmet power needs from times in our life when we were powerless in the face of erratic and sometimes cruel treatment. Too, powerlessness is simply part of growing up, even if your childhood is happy and free of fear. So many of us find ourselves later in life using relationships as an arena in which to work out power issues.

In power struggles, our bodies act out the fear of scarcity: there's never enough to go around. It is a leftover problem from the time in our lives when we were developing our relationship to rules and authority. Many couples get stuck in a stance where arms are crossed and heels are dug in: I'm not going to play.

Susan Campbell, in her interviews with one hundred couples reported in *The Couples' Journey*, found that power struggles blocked most couples from going ahead into a stage of co-creativity. In other words, many couples get bogged down in wrestling with power issues and do not get to a level of closeness that would allow them to create something new for themselves and the world. How to get beyond power struggles is the subject of a later chapter.

Conflicting Feelings

Sometimes in getting close to another person, feelings such as fear, anger, and sadness will arise unbidden from within us. Where do they come from? Did the other person cause them? Why are they coming up now?

The purifying effect of love and positive attention in a relationship will often cause long-harbored feelings to rise to the surface. For example, a man told the authors of a process that concerned him greatly. At the peak of making love with his wife he would find himself thinking angry thoughts about his mother. He would sometimes replay childhood situations that had occurred more than thirty years before. In the process of counseling, he discovered that he had gotten his sexual feelings intertwined with angry feelings toward his mother. Now, when he would feel deep sexual feelings toward his wife, the old anger would be tugged up along with the sexuality. After he allowed himself to feel and explore the old anger, it stopped coming up to cloud his sexual feelings.

The same process can happen with fear and sadness. Somehow they get tied up with the experience of closeness, so that later in life we get close and feel scared or sad. These conflicting feelings must be sorted out carefully. Chances are they have little or nothing to do with the person you are in relationship with in the present. Perhaps the person reminds you of someone from the past, or perhaps it is simply because they are the same gender as the person with whom you originally had the problem. The other person is usually only a trigger for the feelings that bother you.

17

Unexperienced and unexpressed feelings get stored in the body. Like the strings of a harp, these feelings vibrate when a particular chord is struck by getting close to someone. If in the past, for example, you had your feelings misunderstood and turned against you, the current experience of getting close is likely to twang the strings of sadness and fear. Exploring the life of the body, the subtle ways our insides speak to us, can help us in sorting out conflicting feelings so we can clear the channels for closeness.

Arguments

As we get closer to another person, our fears of intimacy may cause us to start an argument or see to it that the other person starts one. But what if the other person actually starts one all by himself or herself? What if we actually are the victim in the situation? The answers to these questions are tough, but potentially illuminating.

In fact, we get to know how much responsibility for an argument belongs to us and how much belongs to the other person only after we have opened ourselves up to the possibility that it's all ours. In other words, after you are willing to acknowledge that the problem may all be a projection of yours, you get a more accurate picture of who actually owns the problem.

For example, a man accuses his wife of having a wandering eye. He says that she flirts with other men when they are out in public. She says, on the other hand, that he is paranoid on the subject, that he sees flirtation when she is only having a normal conversation with another man. Whose problem is it? Looking beneath the surface, we find that his mother left his father and him when he was eight to go off with another man. Ah, so it's his problem! But wait, her father molested her as a child, forcing her into a pattern with men in which she is seductive with a lot of underlying anger.

The point of this example is that there is never any satisfying way to pin a problem to one person in a two-person relationship. The only solution is for both people to take on the problem as their own. Then it becomes possible to know more about how to solve it.

The magic moment in couples therapy comes when two people drop a power struggle ("It's your problem!" "No, it's not, it's yours!") and individually begin to take responsibility for creating the problem. The authors have found that in relationship therapy one person will often take personal responsibility for problems before the other person does. If the other person remains tenaciously attached to blame and fault, there is very little likelihood the relationship will grow. Taking responsibility is so powerful that if one person does and the other doesn't, a volatile situation is at hand.

Illness

Sometimes a movement toward closeness can bring up such deep resistance that the person will become ill in order to pull back. It is common for people to get sick to keep from doing something they have mixed feelings about. A sore throat before a recital, a slipped disc before a vacation—you have probably heard of many such examples. Since the act of getting close brings up such powerful emotions, it is easy to see why we might make ourselves sick rather than experience the intensity of feeling. As an experiment, think of the last few times you were sick. Did they coincide with getting close or getting separate from someone?

One of the authors' favorite examples comes from a friend of ours in California. She and her boyfriend had gone steady through college but had waited until marriage to make love to each other. This was a decision they had agonized over at length because they felt a strong attraction to each other. Finally they graduated and had the Big June Wedding. While they were on their way to a secluded Oregon cabin after the wedding, in heated anticipation of the big moment, a hubcap came off the car and rolled into the bushes. He went to fetch it, got poison ivy from head to toe, and spent the next three days in the hospital with a 103-degree fever. Part of the time he had to be packed in ice

The Experience of Getting Close

There are several key steps involved in getting close. First is your decision that this is really what you consciously want. Not all of us have this as a goal in our lives. If you do, though, the conscious setting of an intention is a potent step. The next step is the process of dealing with whatever comes up that is in the way, whether it is projection, arguments, conflicting feelings, or other manifestations of resistance. The third step is enhancing your ability to experience positive energy. As you clear up your resistances to having close relationships, you will begin to

19

expand and go higher because you have more love and positive energy coming your way. It takes practice to learn to let in more and more positive energy. While we are quite adept at receiving negative energy (we have usually had considerable practice at it), we do not have as much skill in letting in positive energy. New channels must be opened up to enable us to receive it, feel it thoroughly, and learn to express it. We shall discuss the specifics of building channels for positive energy in Chapter 9.

three
On Getting Separate

We hunger for true autonomy as much as we hunger for closeness. On the surface, separateness does not seem like it would be such a good thing as closeness. In fact, it is the essential other half. Our resistance to autonomy is based on the fact that we often associate it with aloneness or loneliness; these latter feelings, however, arise from incomplete separateness. True autonomy comes only after one has eliminated the barriers of loneliness.

A close, truly enlightening relationship can take place only between two people who are also willing to be completely separate. It is a paradox, and an important one to understand.

Human beings have a pulsation in regard to relationships. As in breathing, there is an out-breath and an in-breath. We like to get close, and we like to be autonomous. We often fear both.

Imagine that you are an infant. You seek closeness; you thrive on it. It feeds you. Of course, if your mother does not like you, or is angry at having had you, or is scared, or chain-smokes, you may develop some resistance to getting close combined with your desire for it. Later in life these resistances may rise to the surface when you get close to others.

As you grow as a child, you begin to seek autonomy. You need to develop a sense of self, an ability to feel deeply at home in your own body and in the world. It is crucial to you to learn to explore the world, to stand on your own two feet, to have your own relationship with the universe.

Ideally we would learn to abandon ourselves to total closeness with others, and we would learn to experience total autonomy so that our closeness would not be based on neediness. In fact, few of us achieve this ideal without first doing some serious work on ourselves.

As we get close, we often get afraid of losing our independent sense of self. And up come all the resistances we discussed in the last chapter. As we move toward separateness, we usually have to go through the fear of loneliness to get there. We get worried that we won't be able to get close again, so we pull back from being truly autonomous. Caught in this seesaw of reactions, our ideal flowing dance of full closeness and true autonomy becomes rigid and jerky.

All the problems that come up when we are getting close can also emerge when we are moving toward autonomy. A few examples from the authors' experience follow:

- A man plans a trip by himself to get some space from his family only to injure himself the night before.

- A woman goes back to college after ten years only to get pregnant her first semester.

- A woman leaves her abusive husband only to total her car the first week, leaving her dependent on him for transportation.

Examples like these are common because we fear true dependence. Autonomy is often a particular problem for women, who must contend with such cultural myths as the following:

- A woman is not complete without a man.

- A woman must passively wait, like Sleeping Beauty, until the right man comes along.

- Independence is a masculine trait—a really feminine woman is dependent and semihelpless.

Myths like these have kept women from figuring out what they want and need, and from acting to fulfill their own sense of destiny.

But the fact is that all human beings must struggle with inhibitions and prohibitions against true autonomy. In part we have to overcome what Alan Watts called the taboo against knowing who we are. In large part, though, it is simply a matter of practice and learning. We do not get much training in how to be fully independent. So it is a project that intelligent people have to initiate for themselves. When we are first tuning in to what it will take to be autonomous, the signals come in weakly if at all. Later, with courageous practice, it often becomes easier as the internal information surfaces in a clearer fashion. To start the process, ask yourself several questions:

- "Am I afraid that if I become truly autonomous it will keep me from getting close?"
- "Am I willing to be at once truly autonomous and totally close to others?"
- "What do I need to clear up to become autonomous?"

Questions like these do not have single right answers; rather, they are ways of opening up to a healing, enlightening dialogue with your inner self.

four
The Differences Between a Relationship and an Entanglement

When we first start waking up to what life and relationships are all about, we often realize that we have created a number of entanglements instead of relationships. Entanglements are based on need, incompleteness, and inequality. Relationships are between equals. Often, entanglements are what we have to start with. It is up to us to transform our entanglements into relationships if we are able, and to create new relationships that reflect what we truly want.

Very few of us know how to create enlightening relationships from the beginning. Usually what happens is that one day we wake up, find ourselves deep in entanglements, then go through the often painful process of ending entanglements and creating relationships that truly nourish us.

Here is one man's experience:

My first wife and I were married in our early twenties, at a time when I was probably the most un-conscious I have ever been. I knew next to nothing about myself, my feelings, her feelings, how to communicate; in short, I had none of the skills I would later come to find essential in living my life. A few years later, as the result of counseling, I began to wake up to the world of feelings within myself, to what I wanted and needed, to what I wanted to become. And I gazed in horror at the relationships I was in, particularly the one with my wife. We rarely talked about anything important. We lied to each other frequently, fought bitterly and often, had little in common, and never got beyond our conditioned patterns to deal with anything significant between us.

I had gotten into the relationship because of my old unconscious wants and needs. Looking back, I realize I created a relationship with lies and anger in it because I thought that was the way life was. I was completely out of touch with myself, particularly my anger; perhaps I created such an angry partner to bring me squarely into contact with it.

Leaving the relationship did not solve the problem. After we split up, it still took years of work to clean up all the unfinished business we had amassed in our four years together. I can see now, though, that everything I experienced, awful though it was at the time, was absolutely essential to teach me what I needed to know. My present relationship, and the joy and clarity it has, would not have been possible without the things I learned back then.

CHARACTERISTICS OF ENTANGLEMENTS

In an entanglement you are trying to get something from the other person that you did not get from a past relationship. For example, if you suffered as a child because you could not get the approval you wanted from your father, you might create a relationship with a man from whom it is hard to get approval. Or, if you spent energy as a child keeping Mom happy so she wouldn't get angry, you are now the peacemaker in your present family, always trying to reconcile warring factions.

It never works. Even if you are successful at meeting the old need in the present relationship, something about it never feels quite right. There is part of us that needs to replay old drama, but there is part of us that wants more than that. Ultimately we want to be free of the past, to create something new in ourselves and the universe. That is why we must get beyond entanglements.

A second sign of an entanglement is that you must arrange for the other person to act in ways that match your expectations. A woman mentioned in counseling that her husband always flirted with other women. She cited as an example an experience at a party, when he had told a sexy joke to another woman. "But you were right there," he sputtered, "and you brought her over to meet me in the first place." Upon inquiring into the problem, the woman recalled being witness as a child to numerous battles about her father's infidelities. She sided with her mother in these fights. Later, although her husband was in fact completely faithful to her, she would set up situations in which she could read potential infidelity.

It is not easy to spot these patterns quickly. Sometimes people need to run them by a few thousand times before they see what they are doing. Some, of course, never wake up. They continue to recycle the same patterns throughout their lives.

Sometimes, too, it is not a matter of getting the person to act in ways that match our expectations; rather, we pick a person who fits the required picture without needing any adjustments. For example, a woman ended a hard-fought fifteen-year entanglement with an abusive and alcoholic husband, only to marry an abusive man with a drug problem a few years later.

Another reason we get into entanglements is to complete something that is missing from ourselves. Here are some examples:

- I am out of touch with my feelings, so I get into an entanglement with someone who is highly emotional.

- I cannot love myself, so I link up with someone who assures me I am lovable.

- I am ambivalent about my sexuality, so I link up with someone who has very low sex drive.

One characteristic of entanglements is that they involve making a deal with the other person. Some examples of deals are:

- I'll do the thinking if you do the feeling.
- If you won't change, I won't either.
- If you agree not to talk about _____, then I won't talk about _____

These deals are usually entirely unconscious. If a deal is consciously made ("I'll do the dishes and you mow the lawn, okay?" "Okay."), then it does not present a problem. The deals that cause trouble are

31

those that are based on patterns learned in the past and now being employed unconsciously.

Many people enter relationships seeking completion in some fashion. We want the other person to make up for some lack we feel in ourselves. Another way of saying this is that we often demand from others what we cannot give ourselves; for example, a man who feels unlovable requires frequent assurances of his lovableness by his mate; a woman who is highly dependent requires that her man always be strong and not reveal his tender side.

Relationships based on incompletion and inequality do not serve to enlighten people. Notice what happens when you multiply one-half times one-half. You get one-fourth, less than the value of either multiplier alone. Even if you are seeking just a tiny bit of completion from the other person (nine-tenths times nine-tenths), you still get less than you had before.

Another characteristic of an entanglement is that it is difficult for one person to let the other go through complete cycles of emotion and energy. Entanglements are based on incompletion, so we cannot allow the other person to become complete for fear the relationship would be over. When the partner feels sad, for example, it is hard to let the person go deeply into it to have a complete experience of sadness. We are compelled to rush in and make them feel better. One of the most striking aspects of couple counseling is watching how people block each other from experiencing feelings or telling the truth. Here are a few examples witnessed firsthand:

- A woman begins to talk about some anger she is feeling, and her husband breaks into a fit of coughing. She begins again when he subsides; this time he gets up and asks where the bathroom is.

- A man starts to tell his wife his point of view on a problem; she "spaces out" and has to have it repeated several times.

- A couple finally begin to tell each other the truth about some long-held-back feelings. Then they cancel their next session at the last minute. The following week the therapist gets a note that says they are quitting therapy altogether.

One of the clearest signs of entanglement, then, is that it is hard for one person to let the other person feel his or her feelings and tell the truth about them. The reason for this problem is that in an entanglement we have intermingled our own unfelt feelings and untold truths with the other person's. Instead of consciously agreeing that the relationship exists for the purpose of each person's getting freedom from his or her old feelings and patterns, we create an entanglement by unconsciously agreeing to keep the other person from feeling and expressing certain things. When the other person feels fear, for example, we rush in to assuage it and make it all better.

In the relationship workshops conducted by the authors, we have partners practice simply "being there" while the other person goes through cycles of emotion. We also have people practice listening while their partners verbalize emotions:

- "I'm scared."
- "I'm angry."
- "I want to grow."
- "I'm sad."
- "I'm full of positive energy."
- "I'm happy."

Most people find it very difficult at first to keep from jumping in to interrupt, to give advice, or to provide an instant solution. As humans we get very little training in how to give other people the space to feel and express their feelings.

Most of the time when people tell others what they are feeling, they really don't want advice, solutions, or reassurances that they are right to feel that way. They simply want to be heard, to have their point of view acknowledged. Most people are capable of thinking up their own solutions if they are given a little room in which to do it. The trouble is that many of us have been intruded upon so many times with other people's solutions to our problems, that our own problem-solving skills have never been developed.

In an entanglement, control is a big issue. We want to control how our partners feel, whom they like, what they want. It is important for us to know who they are talking to on the phone and what they get in the mail. Yet in order to have enlightening relationships, each person must learn to let go of control, both of themselves and of the other person, so that they can discover the creativity that comes with freedom.

A final characteristic of entanglement that we will discuss has to do with how conflict is handled. In an entanglement, arguments are often about making one person wrong and the other one right. Both people are trying to prove that they are the victims in the situation, that the other person is the perpetrator. This point of view is based on inequality, so naturally it will never work. But that often does not stop us from engaging in the who's-right—who's-wrong game. It takes practice to learn to solve problems so that both people come out as equals.

Enlightening relationships are based on incompletion and inequality; therefore, they are not characterized by the problems we have discussed in this chapter. At the moment you decide to become whole in yourself and equal to everyone else, any entanglement can be transformed into an enlightening relationship. Just how this process is begun is the subject of our next chapter.

five
How to Create Enlightening Relationships

Enlightening relationships, those that yield ever-increasing clarity and creativity in both partners, grow from certain key intentions in yourself and certain key agreements with your partner. If you are not in a close relationship and desire to be, the setting of correct intentions is probably the single most important step you can take to open you to getting what you want. If you are in a close relationship and want to enlighten it, setting intentions and making meaningful agreements with your partner are the primary tasks that need to be done.

An *intention* is a mindset that makes a difference. For example, one person may say "Hi!" with the intention of wishing you well and another person may say "Hi!" with the intention of snatching your purse. Your intention is the mindset that is behind everything you say and do.

An *agreement* is something that you and your partner agree upon consciously. An agreement is the opposite of a deal, which is usually unconscious and based on inequality. In a deal, for example, a computer programmer who thinks well but is very out of touch with her feelings links up with an opera singer who is highly emotional but has few logical thinking skills. Their unconscious deal is that she will do the thinking if he does the feeling. He will keep her from having to learn about the emotional world, and she will keep him from having to learn to think rationally. In an agreement, they would each spot their respective weaknesses and get the other's support in learning from each other so they could be whole.

SOME TROUBLESOME INTENTIONS

Some people, as we have seen, enter a relationship to complete something from the past, perhaps to get the approval they did not get from a parent. This intention blocks the possibility of their having an enlightening relationship with their current partner, because it is based on the past. If you have a problem with a parent, you cannot hope to resolve it with your present partner. You have to go back into the past, confronting the parent either in your imagination or in real life, and clear up the problem with the person it directly involves.

People also come into relationships with the intention of proving something to themselves or others. We have all sorts of things we are trying to prove:

- "I need to prove I'm lovable."
- "I need to prove I deserve to be here."
- "I need to prove I'm powerful."
- "I need to prove that people can't be trusted."
- "I need to prove my sexuality."
- "I need to confirm that I am stupid and helpless."

All of these issues are crucial to resolve; however, none of them can be proved through a relationship. For example, a man in his twenties had numerous sexual partners but felt unable to make a commitment to any one person. He finally realized that he was trying to prove his sexuality. He'd had a lot of homosexual feelings as a teenager, and some part of his mind was deeply worried that women did not turn him on sexually. Another part of his mind came up with the solution of having a great many sexual partners in order to eliminate his fear. This solution was indirect, however, and gave him no lasting satisfaction. Often a problem does not disappear until it is met directly. For example, a new set of clothes can be a boost to the self-esteem, but to achieve more lasting change we first have to ask ourselves: Why don't I feel good about myself in the first place?

The man with doubts about his sexuality ultimately had to acknowledge his homosexual feelings and the fact that he still had them sometimes. Once he was honest with himself he found that women did, in fact, interest him sexually. Finally, he was able to make a commitment to a woman with whom he later had a child.

Another intention that causes trouble in relationships is the need to be right. Many of us have had the experience in growing up of seeing people around us put a great deal of energy into being right, even if it meant they had to sacrifice the quality of life for themselves and others around them. Naturally, when one person has to be right, someone else has to be wrong. Many of us have learned, then, a way of seeing the world as a place where there is a constant dance of inequality going on. If I'm right, you have to be wrong; if I'm wrong, you must be right. Or, we're both right, and the rest of the world is wrong.

Good judgment gets replaced by judgmentalness; all of our actions have to be filtered through an intention to be right or to protect ourselves from being wrong. Until this need is taken care of, the brakes are on as far as any further development of the relationship is concerned. To begin to eliminate this problem, it is enough to set a new intention: I am now willing to put my energy into being happy and making a contribution to people's lives instead of putting my energy into being right. With this new mindset, your thoughts and actions will begin the slow process of change that will ultimately affect every area of your life.

Another troublesome intention is the one in which we play out a certain script that we unconsciously have adopted as our personal drama. One example is the experience of one of the authors (GH):

My father was overweight, smoked heavily, and did not exercise. He died when he was thirty-two, leaving my mother with an infant (me) to bring up. Later, in my twenties, I was one hundred pounds overweight, smoked heavily, and did not exercise. I did not see the connection between my father's life and mine until one day someone asked me why I was so fat. I realized after much soul-searching that I was replaying my father's life. If I died I would leave my infant daughter behind to be raised by my wife. To top it all off, I was married at the time to a woman whose father had died when she was a child (he was overweight, smoked heavily, did not exercise), leaving her mother to raise her alone. All these awarenesses triggered a turnaround in me which led to my losing the one hundred pounds, stopping smoking, and getting into good physical shape.

There are as many variations in scripts as there are people to play them out. Some themes, however, are common enough to stand out. For example, one common script among women is the one in which a woman is raised to be the perfect representative of a certain ideal. She may find herself later in life with the perfect home, the perfect number of children, and the perfect husband, only to feel perfectly miserable inside. Another common role is that of the man scripted to be the big winner on the gridiron of life, who finds himself at age forty having won big on the outside, only to have a major war going on inside of him.

One reliable way of finding out what script you are playing out is to inquire into it. Ask yourself, your friends, and your family if they see any connection between the way you are living and what they know of your experiences when you were growing up. Not all aspects of scripts cause problems. You will surely want to maintain the parts that work. But you also will never be quite satisfied until you consciously have chosen your life for yourself, rather than running along tracks laid down for you by someone else.

We have seen how intentions and agreements are the starting points for enlightening relationships. Your revised personal intentions and what you and your partner consciously agree upon can be the rules for a liberating new game. We have also explored some of the intentions that do not work to bring about enlightening relationships.

Now, let us proceed to the specific intentions and agreements that make enlightening relationships possible.

six
The Intentions and Agreements Essential to an Enlightening Relationship

One powerful thing about intentions is that you can change them simply by changing your mind. Intentions exist only in the mind, although they influence everything we say and do. Because they are purely in the mind, intentions can be changed as quickly and completely as you can change your mind. For example, all your life you may have been operating with the intention of getting love from people in relationship with you. One day you wake up, see the folly of that position, and decide to change your intention. You think: From now on I am going to focus on *giving* love to people in relationship with me. The change has been made entirely in your own mind, and yet it alters everything. No doubt there will be a period of going back and forth between the old intention (getting love) and the new intention (giving love). But once you have set a new intention, there is no way you can go back entirely to your previous mindset. So you shouldn't be surprised if your actions begin to change radically in the new direction.

There is the same kind of beautiful simplicity to agreements. If you come up with an enlightening intention, all you have to do is ask your partner if he or she will consciously agree to have it be part of your relationship.

When you set an enlightening intention or make an enlightening agreement with your partner, you often invite into your awareness anything that is in the way of it. So, for example, the day after you set the intention "I'm now willing to clear up my fear of death," you may see death and decrepitude everywhere. Similarly, you and your partner may make an agreement, "Our relationship is going to be about celebrating our full potential rather than holding each other back." The next minute, your deepest power struggle may reveal itself in disquieting detail. Of course, sometimes the new intention slides easily into place without stirring up any resistance to itself.

Here are some of the intentions and agreements that have been found useful in bringing about personal freedom and enlightening relationships. As you read them, please feel free to try them on in your mind so that you can notice what resistance they stir up. If you are in a close relationship, you may want to seek agreement from your partner on some of the ones that appeal to you most.

The intentions are in the form of "I'm willing . . ." statements. The reason for this is that when you are willing for a change to occur, without demanding that it occur in a certain way, you open up tremendous creative possibilities. For example, if you lose your keys and "try" to find them, it is often very frustrating. This is because you are making an effort to find them, and probably using the same state of mind you were in when you lost them. If you relax and simply get willing to find them, you move from an effortful focus to a wider perspective. The moment we become willing for something to happen without demanding that it happen in a certain way, we move beyond the restrictions of normal ego consciousness. The ego is an important part of us, but it is only a part of us; there are many more creative ways the mind can operate. Willingness allows us to stand free of the limitations of the mind so that a deeper creativity can emerge. At first it may feel odd to solve problems and make changes without ego and effort. That is because we have come to expect change to be hard. Let us experiment with a new way, though, to see if it serves us better.

INTENTION #1

I am willing to be totally independent and totally close. Establishing this intention in your mind sets a new game for you to play. The old game looked something like this:

We get close, and up comes fear of losing self. So we make ourselves or our partner wrong in order to have an excuse to pull back. Then we get separate, and up comes fear of being alone, of not experiencing unity. So we get sick, or pull some manipulation to get close again.

The solution to this problem is for both people to agree to be totally close, and to give each other total permission to become fully independent.

INTENTION #2

I am willing to have my relationships be a force that takes me to full enlightenment. All of us have our own definitions of what enlightenment is. For one person, it is simply getting free of some troublesome pattern. For another person, it is blissful union with the Divine. Regardless of your definition, this intention allows your relationships to serve your enlightenment. For thousands of years many people have thought that human relationships detract from enlightenment. Yogis go to caves, monks to monasteries, nuns to convents. Some theologians have often implied that if you really want to serve spiritual growth you have to eliminate sex and close relationships with the opposite sex. It is now time to heal this split and see the truth of the matter: With the correct intentions, relationships can enhance spiritual growth. If we view other people as equals, then our relationships with them become as important to enlightenment as meditation, prayer, postures, books, or rituals. All things, we must remind ourselves, are connected to all other things. So if we withdraw from relationships with people, we are in fact withdrawing from enlightenment itself.

INTENTION #3

I am willing to clear up anything in the way of my full enlightenment and ability to be close. This is a key intention that can allow your journey to enlightenment to become much smoother. If you develop the intention of clearing up any personality issues that stand between you and full enlightenment and closeness, you ignite a rocket underneath your life. Then, if you are willing to carry out the intention with no inconvenience to yourself and others, you reduce drag on yourself and others around you so that the ride becomes much more fun. For example, if part of your enlightenment involves dealing with a lot of old repressed anger inside you, one way to handle it would be to punch a few people out. Doing it this way might inconvenience you, though, and it would almost certainly inconvenience others. In contrast, you could discharge the anger by chopping wood or having a furious workout at the gym, and no one would be inconvenienced by it.

This intention is one of the deepest commitments we can make to ourselves and each other. It is in contrast to some of the commitments we perhaps have made in the past:

- Will you stick with me no matter how badly I abuse myself and you?
- Will you deny your growth if I deny mine?
- Will you set new records for pain endurance on my behalf?

With Intention #3, you make it clear to yourself and others that you are committed to your transformation and to the highest development of your relationships. You are on record as being willing to transform in ways that simultaneously serve you and the people around you. In enlightening relationships, there can be no conflict between what serves your evolution and what serves your relationships as a whole. If both parties are agreed that their growth and the relationship's growth are the same, even seeming conflicts can be viewed as contributing to the growth of the relationship. This way of thinking is radically different from that which most of us have seen around us in our development.

INTENTION #4

I am willing to have other people be fully empowered in my presence. Some people base their relationships on unconscious deals that limit the other person's power and potential. The unspoken contract is: I'll stay in this relationship with you as long as you don't become too powerful, creative, and independent. This deal is a holdover from the "Who's boss?" struggles in childhood.

The intention to allow others to be powerful and successful in your presence announces to those around you that you are willing to support their highest well-being. It often has the effect of forcing others to think about what they want and need to live out their full potential. When people in a close relationship agree that they are there to support each other's full development, a most creative alliance is formed.

INTENTION #5

I'm willing to take space as often as necessary to nurture myself and the relationship. In a close relationship it is necessary to be conscious about taking time off. Human beings need time and space to themselves, away from close contact with others. If we do not get an occasional respite from contact with others, we have a tendency to lose contact with our inner selves. When this contact with the inner self is lost, it is easy to slip into resentment, blame, and a lessened sense of responsibility for our lives. If we do not allow ourselves to take space consciously, we will usually find a way to do it unconsciously, often through getting sick, having an accident, or starting an argument to alienate others.

Human beings seem to have as great a need for space as they do for closeness. It takes conscious work in a relationship to let it be all right for both people to take time off from each other. It seems essential to do so, though, particularly in an enlightening relationship where both people are growing and changing constantly.

INTENTION #6

I am willing to have our relationship be about giving and receiving maximum positive energy. When you choose an enlightening relationship, you consciously design a new game. The old games are very familiar to us. The old games are about things like:

- Power struggles
- Accumulating goods
- Putting on a good show for the neighbors

47

- Suffering and sacrifice
- Staying together for the children
- Regrets and resentments, mutually shared and repressed.

Enlightening relationships create some vibrant new rules for the game. One of the finest things relationships can be about is giving and receiving the maximum amount of positive energy. It is possible to decide consciously that your relationship is going to be based on exchanging positive energy rather than on things like power struggles, problems, and mutual suffering. The authors have experienced the results personally, have seen them in other people's lives, and recommend the experience highly.

To build enlightening relationships, we have to develop the skill of setting intentions that simultaneously serve our own evolution and the growth of the relationship. To do so we must be courageous enough to create something entirely new against tremendous pressure from the past. On our side is the fact that the human being is remarkably creative and flexible. Also on our side, it is our deep conviction, is the fact that humans really want enlightening relationships.

When you look your partner in the eye and ask, "Are you willing to have our relationship be about having fun instead of having problems?", chances are you'll get a surprised "Yes!" Whether you get a yes or a rapidly backpedalling partner, at least you will have the clarity and satisfaction of knowing what you want and of being courageous enough to speak up in its behalf.

seven
What Entanglements Look and Feel Like in the Body

When they walked in for their first counseling session, tension crackled between them like electricity. She moved with a jerky quickness, glancing over her shoulder at him as he dragged his body along. Her eyes flitted as she spoke, fingers flicking, her whole body asquirm. His chest was walled off, breath invisible, face impassive. "What would you like to have happen?" the therapist asked. He replied, "I'd like her not to be so sloppy." She said, "I'd like to be more intimate." Their body language perfectly reflected their problem: They lived in the same house but in two different worlds.

It is important to have an intellectual understanding of how entanglements work. In this chapter, though, we want to go further, into how entanglements look and feel. In order to clear up entanglements and move into enlightening relationships, it is necessary to become an astute observer of the nonverbal aspects of troublesome relationship patterns. The patterns that cause us difficulty in relationships are all visible to the sensitive observer. The patterns appear in the way we carry our bodies, the way we move, the way we breathe, how we hold ourselves as we interact with others.

Exploration of the nonverbal world generates consciousness, dissolving the veil between people so that they can experience and express their feelings, needs, and issues directly. In this chapter we will discuss the common nonverbal issues that trouble people in relationships; the later chapter on nonverbal activities will provide exercises which can put these learnings into practice.

The way one's body moves and feels in the presence of the other reflects exactly what is going on in the relationship. In entanglements, partners' bodies change shape in uncomfortable ways. One shrinks, another puffs the chest. While one partner is talking, the other tilts his or her head and turns slightly away. The body may reflect a conflict between wanting to get close and also fearing it; pelvis and legs may be reaching forward while the shoulders are pulling back. On the other hand, one might want to be close while being afraid of one's sexuality. In this pattern, the chest and shoulders are forward while the pelvis is pulled back.

Controlling the other person is a central problem in entanglements. Control generates intrusive movement patterns. Here are a few classics:

- Interrupting the other person while he or she is speaking
- Moving into the partner's space in a threatening way
- Standing over the other person
- Looking away (perhaps glancing at the clock) during an interchange
- Sighing or fidgeting while the other person is talking

Often, control problems manifest themselves in not allowing partners to complete actions. A sentence is finished for the partner, something dropped by one partner is picked up by the other. Control is also manifested in dragging passively on the relationship. One partner holds back, keeps secrets, walks slower, has trouble getting ready to go out on time, shows up late for luncheon dates. In some cases both partners compete to see who can outdrag the other one.

Too, some people believe that once they are in a committed relationship they have certain unspoken rights over the other person. Examples are the right to know what the other person is thinking, who they are talking to, where they are going. Another form of these rights is the "If you really loved me . . ." expectation. Examples of these unconscious beliefs are "If you really loved me you would want to spend all your free time with me," or "If you really loved me you would dislike the same people I dislike."

These expectations are communicated through body language that is unique to the people involved. For example, one man communicated his expectations about his partner's housekeeping duties by straightening up after she had finished cleaning a room. In another example, a couple would spend an hour or two in the same room without touching each other. Then the phone would ring, and the man would go to answer it. As he carried on his conversation, suddenly his wife would become very affectionate, coming over to hug him and nuzzle his ears as he talked.

If partners cannot speak the truth directly to each other, they have an entanglement. If you cannot seem to tell your partner your feelings, wants, and needs, or if your body feels uncomfortable as you are communicating, there is likely an entanglement that needs straightening out. Body signs of not telling the truth include difficulty in making eye contact, tilting the head, looking out from under the eyebrows, and holding the breath.

Breathing patterns closely reflect one's ability to communicate clearly. For example, a person in therapy discovers a polarity within himself, two separate personalities that he would dial up as the situation demanded. One personality's body language reflected the part of himself he hated: he leaned to the left, held his breath in an inflated chest, pursed his lips severely, and walked in a stiff march. In his other personality, which he called "the martyr," he shifted his weight to the right side of his body, collapsed his middle in a heavy sigh, limped slightly, and dragged his body in meandering circles. Both personalities expressed his conflict over needing and wanting attention but being terrified of actually getting close to people.

In some entanglements, partners feel that they can't get enough breath. We often stop ourselves from feeling by stopping breathing fully. If you notice yourself feeling short of breath, or not having "breathing space," or yawning a lot around your partner, this may indicate that there are some entanglements that need unraveling. Perhaps you are stuck in some old pattern, or perhaps there is a withheld truth that needs telling.

The body speaks its own language. Here are some examples of the body communicating messages that the mind and mouth have not yet said. A woman who doesn't really want to go on vacation with her husband strains her back the night before they're to leave. A man gets a headache the afternoon of their regular dance club evening. A head is banged on a shelf a few minutes after some anger is repressed during an argument.

Our bodies have an intelligence all their own. If we learn to listen to them, they can tell us a great deal about what is going on at deeper levels of our being. In relationships where people have trouble speaking the truth directly to each other, there are a great many more body complaints, accidents, and illnesses.

SPACE, WEIGHT, AND TIME

Now we will explore three issues that cause many problems in relationships: space, weight, and time. Each of these issues has nonverbal components that can be very illuminating when properly understood.

Space

Here are several scenarios that illustrate common problems with regard to the use of space in a relationship.

- She wants to talk over some problems. He agrees and suggests that they do so in the family room after dinner. When she comes in, the room is full of smoke from his cigarette. She is allergic to cigarette smoke, and he has agreed not to smoke in the house.

- A man goes to hug his wife. She shrinks away and goes back to reading. Then, just as he is getting involved with working in his study, she comes in and tries to get his attention.

- He lies down to read. She decides to make a long-distance call to her deaf aunt in the same room.

- They've been on a week's vacation, together twenty-four hours a day. On the way home they get into a huge argument over who gets the window seat on the plane.

Since space issues involve our whole bodies, they are often best uncovered by studying our body language. For example, in the course of therapy the counselor had a couple try an experiment in which they formed shapes in movement as they circled the room. Her movements were all centered around defining a space for herself beyond being a wife and mother. His actions were all directed at rigidly preventing her from finding a space for herself. Their movements perfectly reflected the dramas in which they were engaged in real life. Ultimately she moved out because she could not seem to get the space she needed.

When space issues are needing attention, certain incidents begin to happen:

- Noticing clothes left around
- Asking where "my" book is
- Making sure the pie is evenly divided
- Feeling angry when someone puts an elbow on "my" seat at the movies

One of the clearest signs of entanglement is an uncomfortable fluctuation in the body when the partner gets close or goes away. In other words, your body feels an unpleasant tug when you and your partner come in and out of each other's space. Space issues are ultimately rooted in our old deep fears of getting close and getting separate, so much careful attention must be paid to these issues in order to have enlightening relationships.

Weight

How do you ask for what you want and need in your relationships? Is it easy? Can you do it straightforwardly and clearly? Or do you use aggressive, wily tricks or some other indirect approach? These questions are connected to how we relate to the weight and size of ourselves and others.

Men are generally larger than women. This fact has contributed to many of the scripted roles between the sexes. Such things as paternalism, chivalry, and feminine wiles have grown out of the inequality in size between men and women. Women generally cannot get what they want by brute force, so they have developed a range of persuasive techniques, many nonverbal, to augment their smaller physical size. Makeup, clothing styles, and sexually provocative behavior are part of the arsenal. As one man said to his mate in therapy, "I'm bigger and you can't make me!" "Wanna bet?" she said with a seductive leer.

Inequality and fear between men and women are at the root of this behavior. Throwing one's weight around is often the last resort when being straight has not worked. The enormously high incidence of spousal abuse is a grim testimony to poor resolution of weight and size issues in relationships. For example, one couple had an entanglement in which he would not fight with her. To her, fighting was an essential form of contact; it meant he really loved her. When he would not respond, she would escalate her attack; one time she started pounding on him as he sat woodenly in the chair. When he would reach out to her in his preferred manner of contact, she would act distracted and scattered.

Power struggles are often weight issues. Do we withhold our impact in the relationship? Do we go passive and slack? Do we steamroller our partners? In these and other related issues, the essential body language to be observed is how we handle weight and size. It is well worth observing yourself in relationships to notice if you get smaller with certain people or inflate yourself in the presence of others. The best arena to watch the play of weight and size issues is in your body language: your gestures, your postures, the way you move through the world.

Time

Time is a subtle influence on relationships, at once so shadowy and so pervasive that we often overlook its dramatic effects on our interactions.

Each of us has a preferred rhythm for moving through life. This rhythm is deeply ingrained in us. Some of us buzz like bees through life, others saunter. In entanglements, we often are made to feel wrong for our particular rhythm. "Hurry up! We haven't got all day," says one partner to another. "Do you always have to rush through everything?" the other replies.

One sign of an entanglement is one or both partners criticizing the other's rhythm. In therapy one day, the therapist was having a couple walk around the room together. The purpose of the activity was to notice what type of compatibility each had with the other's rhythm. Within seconds, he began to criticize her for moving too quickly. She became furious. After some exploration of the problem, it emerged that he was afraid of her rhythm. He associated her quickness with loss of control and was afraid that she would become scattered and manic. His slowness was a point of irritation with her; it reminded her of her infuriatingly methodical father.

When people ignore or deny their natural rhythms, problems can emerge. For example, a woman always got up at 6 A.M. to make breakfast for her husband, even though she secretly hated doing it. Often she would burn something or have some other kitchen mishap occur. Upon exploring the situation, she realized that she was a night person, while her husband was a morning person. They solved the problem by her making some tasty breakfasts the night before that he could fix up quickly. It turned out that he actually preferred to spend the morning time by himself instead of contending with a disgruntled and barely awake partner.

One of the deals that is often made in entanglements is that partners feel they have to take on the other's rhythm. Sometimes this time-change is successful, but more often the body stages some sort of protest. We protest by getting sick, having accidents, and starting arguments, as well as in many other ways. In one relationship, the woman liked to read and rest at night. She could easily sit for several hours in the living room without moving much at all. He, on the other hand, was much more active. At first, because he liked to be with her, he tried sitting with her and reading, too. He lasted about three nights, then exploded at her for being so "lazy." Eventually, after much negotiation, they worked out a compromise in which they gave each other space to occupy their own rhythms. Other couples do not accomplish this key task, and the relationship founders.

The solution to the time problem is twofold. First each of us has to inquire within and find out what rhythm suits us best. This step is not easy, because we all have had many experiences of being talked out of our natural rhythms. Once we are in touch with how we like to pulsate, the next task is either to attract people who share the same rhythm, or to give space to people to have their own rhythms in our presence.

Becoming aware of the nonverbal signs of entanglements can be a powerful practice. The body and its movements are a direct readout of the unconscious. The mouth can tell outrageous lies, but the body speaks the truth. So, to disentangle ourselves and create enlightening relationships, we need to become sharp observers of the ways our bodies feel and move as we interact with the people around us. As your skill in this area grows, be prepared for some exhilarating (and often humbling!) awarenesses.

eight
Projection:
a Major Barrier
to Enlightening
Relationships

Projection begins the moment we forget we are in charge of creating the experience we are having. When we are projecting, we pretend that other people and the world are responsible for our thoughts, feelings, and the events that befall us. Projection comes in many forms. Here are some real-life examples of projection in action:

- A man accuses his wife of flirting with other men at a party. A battle ensues. When it is all thrashed out a week later, it emerges that he had felt a lot of sexual feelings for a woman at the party, had suppressed those feelings, and then had become obsessed with the sexual quality of his wife's interactions with other men.

- A woman upbraids her partner for being overly critical. Later she realizes that she has a loud inner voice that sneers at her every adventurous step.

- You have a number of encounters with angry people before you suddenly realize that you are carrying around a lot of anger. After your realization, the angry people disappear.

A woman at a workshop given by the authors gave a perfect example of how projection works. Recently divorced after a long marriage, she was beginning to make her own way in the world. She prided herself on being a model citizen, never having received a traffic ticket, so when a policeman pulled her over one day she was astounded. She insisted that she couldn't possibly have been speeding: "I just don't do things like that." Unmoved by this point of view, the policeman gave her a ticket anyway. A week later she got another ticket, again from a male policeman, for the same offense. Again she argued righteously to no avail. A month later, when she got her third ticket, she woke up and asked herself: Am I the one that's angry? Do I have some issues to work out with male authority figures? She discovered a deeply held and fierce anger at her ex-husband that she had never dealt with. Going into it more deeply, she traced it back to feelings she also had toward her father and grandfather. She also saw how holding onto the anger was limiting her success in her career. As soon as she explored the feelings and cleared them up, her career took a quantum jump in a more positive direction.

Projection can also take the form of not claiming for ourselves a positive quality that we see in abundance in someone else. Competitive feelings often stem from seeing something that we admire in another person and want for ourselves. Instead of opening up to it and being willing to have it in our own life, we often retire into defeat and competitive thoughts such as, "Oh, well, I wouldn't really want to be like that," or "He probably tromped on a lot of people to get where he is."

In a similar way, we often project onto our relationships something that is actually an issue inside ourselves. For example, if I need to open up and claim more of my power, and if I'm afraid to do that, I may begin to notice how much the relationship I'm in is limiting me. I begin to notice how much power my partner has and how it is keeping me oppressed.

One facet of projection that is almost always present in entanglements is the working out of one's internal male and female issues in the relationship. All of us, whether we're man or woman, must develop the male and female within us. Each of us must develop a healthy relationship with those traits traditionally considered feminine: feelings, intuition, compassion, an all-embracing view of life. Too, each of us must develop the masculine principle within us: the outgoing, expressive, problem-solving, specific function. A whole man is in touch with his feelings; a whole woman is at home expressing herself in the world. Most of us have a great deal of work to do to perfect the development of the male and female consciousness within us. When we are out of balance, we may try to make ourselves whole by linking up with a person who represents what we do not have. A man, for example, may need to learn to be more in touch with his feelings and needs. He may connect with a woman who is very emotional and needy; then he may complain about what he's got. It may not occur to him that she is simply a reflection of something he needs to open up to in himself. Similarly, a woman may not be willing to cultivate the assertive, outgoing part of herself that the masculine principle represents. So she may project onto the relationship and think, "He won't let me be who I really am."

Of course, oftentimes these problems we perceive actually are present in the relationship. But we do not get to confront the problems effectively until we are willing to drop projection and confront them in ourselves.

One of the authors (KH) describes a dream that illustrates the projection of internal male and female issues:

> I awoke one morning feeling sad and suspicious after dreaming that Gay was attracted to another woman and hadn't told me about it. The hangover from the dream made me feel distant from Gay, and I noticed it right away because we usually feel very close. I like to explore dreams by asking myself what part of myself each part of the dream represents. I asked myself what part of me I was feeling distant from. Up came the answer. I was feeling afraid of getting closer, and along with the fear was emerging a deep old mistrust of males. Going further, it felt like the deeper meaning of the dream was that I didn't trust my own internal male, that I did not yet feel comfortable owning my power out in the world. The dream seemed to be a projection of that issue onto my relationship with Gay. So I opened up more to my power, experienced the fear, and talked about the whole thing with Gay. Suddenly I felt close to him, completely in harmony again.

DISSOLVING PROJECTION

The key to dissolving projection is for each person to take 100 percent responsibility for everything that emerges in the relationship. This intention allows all events and feelings that emerge in the relationship to be perfect for your growth at that moment. You get to know what's projection and what's not only after you're willing to consider everything as a projection.

An important step in this process is identifying the cues inside you that will let you know that you're projecting. For example, a woman sneezed often with what she thought were hay fever symptoms. Upon the recommendation of a therapist, she began noticing what she was thinking and feeling just before she sneezed. She started noticing that she sneezed frequently when she was holding back her power or not saying something she wanted to say. A dramatic breakthrough happened one day as she was shopping for a washer and dryer. The purchase had much significance for her; it represented one of the first major purchases of her adult life. At the store she encountered some difficult choices. As she debated whether to make the decision herself or wait and talk it over with her husband, she began to sniffle and sneeze. She went out and sat in her car for a while until she perceived the meaning of the sniffling. Then she went back into the store and made the best choice she could. At the moment she made the decision, her sniffling and sneezing vanished.

When we first realize the enormous power of projection, how deeply it pervades our way of seeing and being in the world, our first response is often outraged denial. It can be infuriating to realize that we have created a reality full of suffering, unpleasantness, and lack of energy. These feelings need to be acknowledged as we loosen our bonds to our old ways of experiencing the world.

Questions that have been found useful by the authors in exploring projection are:

- "Where and how did I learn to see things this way?"
- "What am I feeling in my body?"
- "Do I feel afraid? Angry? Sad?"
- "Do I feel in charge of my feelings right now? If not, who is 'causing' them?"
- "Am I telling the whole truth to myself? To my partner?"
- "Am I taking up my full space? Am I making myself smaller?"
- "What do I want in this situation?"

The experience of projection involves taking a position with one's mind and body. I'm right; it's your fault; you won't let me do what I want; you think you've got it bad. These positions have a direct effect on the body. They stop the flow of energy and fix it in frozen reactions to life. With practice, it is possible to catch projection as it is occurring and to notice how it affects the body. For example, one man began to study his paranoid thoughts, such as "Everybody's out to get me" and "Nobody likes me." He noticed that when he was engaging in those thoughts his head was jutting forward in front of his body. This position would lead to eyestrain and headaches.

A quick way to dissolve projection, then, is to notice thoughts and body feelings that indicate one is not taking full responsibility for one's experience of life. When you have opened up to what is going on beneath the surface of projection, you can more easily love yourself for however you are feeling. Loving some part of yourself, even a part of you that is unpleasant, is often the quickest way to banish projection.

Dissolving projection is a key to clear, truthful, and evolving relationships. You get the opportunity to see things as they are when you drop projection. The world is a luminous, shimmering place, and relationships can be an ecstatic dance when we see through the veil of projection. To evolve, each person must grow toward being the source of love for themselves and others. Whole persons are willing to own the full range of feelings and potential within themselves. They embrace the male and female consciousness that resides within them. The payoff for being nimble enough to drop projection is that they get to ride the waves of energy and aliveness that wholeness brings, and their radiance is apparent to others.

nine
Solving the Upper-Limits Problem: Learning to Handle More Positive Energy

Many of the troubles we encounter in life and in relationships come from running up against upper limits in ourselves and others. A thorough understanding of the upper-limits problem can prevent many of the most irritating snags that humans hit.

Here's how it works. In growing up we learn to limit the amount of energy we feel and express. If your parents are in the midst of an argument when you come in exhilarated with a freshly caught frog, you may hit a wall when you try to communicate your enthusiasm to them. Do you remember any of these phrases from childhood?

- "What are you so happy about?"
- "Don't count your chickens before they hatch."
- "There's many a slip 'twixt the cup and the lip."
- "You think everything's great now, but you just wait until later in life."
- "Be still!"

Slogans like these are often used to warn people of the dangers of getting too excited, of feeling too good, of getting their hopes up. Many families are precariously balanced, so that it doesn't take much energy to upset the system. As children we learn to put upper limits on how good we can feel so that we can survive and keep the system intact.

When we begin as adults to explore ourselves, to experience our feelings and love ourselves, our inner energy starts to build. The increased energy pushes against the limits we have previously learned to live within. As we go beyond our upper limits, we enter a zone we have not occupied before, and fear of the unknown comes up. At this point we often do something to bring ourselves back down into the familiar zone again. Illness and accidents are two of the most popular ways we have of bringing ourselves down when we've exceeded our limits. For example, one man noticed a pattern in his life that had occurred in virtually the same way three times. The interesting thing about the pattern was that the three incidents spanned a period of nearly ten years. When he first broke away from his family at eighteen, he drove from the South to New York. As he left he got a crick in his neck, so he was in pain the whole trip. Seven years later he split up with his wife and drove across the country to California. The night before he left he injured his neck and shoulders while doing a yoga posture. He was unable to move his head without pain during the long drive. Several years after that incident, he left the west coast to drive back east for a new job. Again he injured himself before the trip, making the drive very uncomfortable. It wasn't until the third incident that he spotted the pattern. Upon reflection, he figured out that he had an upper limits problem. Each of the incidents happened when he was about to do what he wanted to do. When he moved toward greater freedom he started feeling better than ever, thus violating his upper limit. The injuries had the effect of bringing him back down into a more familiar zone. After all, he thought, it is not fair for me to feel good if everybody else isn't happy, too.

In relationships the upper-limits problem is compounded. When two people move closer to each other, the energy is multiplied and increased. Imagine that each of us has a hidden thermostat that sets off an unconscious alarm if we go past a certain setting. In a relationship the alarms go off even more easily than when we are alone, due to the increased energy and unpredictability of two people. When the alarms sound, we often do something to bring the relationship back down.

Here are some of the more popular ways of bringing a relationship down:

Projection. For example, you are experiencing some anger but are out of touch with it or do not know how to express it. So you see it in the other person and say, "You look angry about something today." Because projection is so pervasive in relationships, a separate chapter discusses this problem in detail.

Starting an Argument. Arguments are probably the most popular way of dealing with upper limits in relationships. They can happen instantly and can bring both persons down into the familiar zone very quickly. Many people are not acquainted with how the upper-limits problem works, so they do not observe that arguments are a way of bringing the relationship down after the unconsciously agreed-upon limits have been exceeded. If you haven't learned to be aware of the upper-limits problem and how projection works, you may think the other person started the argument. A power struggle then ensues, bringing the relationship's positive energy to a halt.

Fighting for the Victim Position. As you get closer in a relationship, the energy builds and flushes out anything that is creating blocks in either person. Old resentments may bubble up. Regrets and long-stored hurts may come to the surface. These events, remember, are happening because love is working, not because of a lack of love. The problem comes when we forget to take responsibility for the things that are emerging. The moment we start projecting responsibility onto the other person, a race gets underway to see who gets to be the victim in the relationship. Hardly anybody likes to be made the bad guy, so both people have to outdo each other to get to be the victim.

A dialogue between a couple in therapy went like this: (The therapist had asked the man how he felt right then.)

He: I'm unhappy.

She: [breaking in with a snort] You're unhappy! You've got nothing to be unhappy about. You've got it made. I'm the one that's unhappy.

He: How come you think I'm so happy?

She: You got your new truck, didn't you? I haven't got anybody to talk to.

He: I need that truck for work. And besides, I don't have anybody to talk to either.

She: At least you've got a job.

71

On it goes. Once we have started to maneuver toward the victim position, either by thinking "poor me" thoughts or engaging in victim behavior, it is all lost. There is no way to win the game because victims do not win. The best we can hope for is the commiseration of fellow losers.

Going to Sleep. Another popular upper-limits pastime is to go unconscious and begin to run on automatic programs. Instead of increasing self-awareness and aliveness by exploring themselves more deeply, many people opt for a state of comfortable somnolence. They go through life as if sleepwalking, never airing their minds by changing opinions, never transforming their bodies by challenging stereotyped ways of moving through space. For example, one couple would go to sleep when the rising energy between them would bring up old unexpressed anger. Their body language was revealing. She stood with eyes downcast, looking like a four-year-old trying to be good. In response to this behavior, he began yawning and retreating. This pattern escalated into sighs and obvious tiredness. They would go to different parts of the house to recover. As this couple explored their patterns, many liberating awarenesses emerged. Her behavior reminded him of his mother's actions just before she would become irrational and abusive. His seeming disinterest dialed up her memories of her father's impenetrable boredom in response to her childhood liveliness. As is often the case, they had seemingly picked each other to help them work out these ancient patterns.

Not Experiencing Feelings. One way to avoid confronting upper limits is to cut off feeling. You feel angry at someone, for example, and instead of allowing yourself to feel it deeply you cut yourself off from the experience. Or, in a relationship you feel sexual feelings for someone other than your partner. Then you feel guilty and cut yourself off from experiencing the sexual feelings. The trouble is that the act of cutting off feelings deadens us and takes energy out of the relationship. Enlightening relationships thrive on the wholeness of each person, so if one person siphons off energy, both people are cheated.

Not Telling the Truth. One of the most common reasons people hide the truth is to keep from feeling more positive energy than they can handle. A lie stops the flow of positive energy in two ways. If you feel angry about something, for example, and do not share it with your partner, a vapor lock is created in the relationship. Growth cannot resume until the lock is broken and the flow of energy begins again. Another kind of lie occurs when we distort something in the telling of it. If we think of the truth as being like a pure tone, the distortion of it sounds like a discordant note played along beside it. We hear the discord, but do not know quite what to do about it.

In our experience as therapists, we have learned that people are very good at knowing when other people, and they themselves, are lying. But people are astonishingly skillful at pretending not to notice. In our desire to keep things glazed over and looking good, we all conspire to be less perceptive and intuitive when it comes to feeling and telling the truth.

Why do we lie? One reason is that we have been punished for telling the truth. After a few incidents of suffering for telling the truth, the very dullest person will think, "Hey, if illusions are what they want, I'll give 'em illusions." Another reason for lying is that we do not want to wade through the fallout that results from telling the truth. People go through all sorts of emotional acrobatics when they hear the truth; it takes much courage and commitment to ride out the display so that a successful resolution will take place.

Many people have told the authors in therapy that they lie to their partners because the partners would feel bad if they were told the truth. Somehow we come to feel that it's better to let the relationship disappear in a fog of untruth than it is to see the hurt or anger on the other's face. Decreased aliveness always results from untold truth, but this sort of numbness is perhaps easier to handle than a potential explosion from the partner.

There is no trick to telling the truth. Even if you have a life-changing flash of revelation in which you are commanded by the universe to forever speak the truth, it still will take practice. There are activities and experiments in the chapter on communication that many people have found helpful in learning the skill of telling the truth so it gets heard.

Breaking Agreements. A sure way to slow down the flow of positive energy in a relationship is for someone to break an agreement. Not keeping agreements is a very common way to bring down a relationship if the upper limits have been reached. Here are some examples of unkept agreements, both trivial and significant, that have tripped up couples:

- A man agrees to do a household task on a regular basis, but "forgets" to do it. His wife has to remind him frequently to do it.

- A woman agrees not to see her former lover. Analyzing the semantics, she realizes she hasn't agreed not to talk to him on the phone. So she calls him frequently, always feeling guilty afterward, but does not tell her husband about the calls or the guilt.

- A couple has an agreement that they will decide mutually on any social engagements, but one person continues to accept invitations without checking it out with the other.

- With the help of a counselor, a couple agrees to talk about feelings and their relationship every Thursday evening. Every Thursday something seems to come up, though, and they never get around to it.

- A man likes to go out drinking with his buddies. He agrees to be home or call by a certain time. He repeatedly fails to do this, with uproar all around.

There seems to be part of the mind that keeps watch on the agreements we make and whether we keep them or not. Two sure ways to decrease aliveness in a relationship are to (1) make agreements you don't want to make and (2) fail to keep the ones you make. Often it is the seemingly trivial agreements that cause the most trouble. This is because not keeping agreements is a symptom of deeper conflict in a relationship, and it really doesn't matter whether the broken agreement is small or large.

Either you keep agreements or you don't. If you don't, then another key issue arises: whether or not you go back afterward and clean up the broken agreement. Anyone can study the relationship between one's success in relationships and whether one keeps agreements scrupulously. You will be astounded, as the authors have been, at how closely the two are related. When an agreement is broken, a vital part of oneself is removed from the relationship and a block is inserted where the person's energy was. All is not lost if an agreement is broken, however. There is always the option to go back, admit to the broken agreement, and see what needs to be done to fix it up.

There seem to be three main areas of awareness in regard to agreements. The first is noticing what agreements you make, both the conscious and unconscious ones. It is important, for example, to make agreements that you have your heart in, that are meaningful to you. Many agreements are broken because the person made them unwillingly in the first place.

A second skill is the actual carrying of the agreement to completion. For example, if you agree to take out the trash, it also means picking up the papers you knocked over as you were doing the task. The third skill is how you handle things if you don't keep the agreement. Most of the problems that result from broken agreements can be straightened out easily with a few minutes of clear communication. Unfortunately, many people seem to prefer pretending it never happened to performing the act of courage necessary to clean it up.

Too, many people have a special emotion that they think exempts them from the usual laws of the universe. For example, a man had a big problem with anger. Whenever he felt really angry, he used that emotion as his excuse to break agreements all over the place. He and his wife had a monogamy agreement, but when he would get mad at her for something, he would go out for a one-night sexual encounter with someone else. When his anger subsided he would feel guilty. He couldn't bring himself to admit to the broken agreements, though, and the marriage ultimately eroded.

Many people have feelings they think are special:

- "When I am angry then I get to steal and cheat."
- "When I feel really hurt I don't have to tell the truth."
- "When I feel scared I get to overeat."
- "When I'm upset it's okay to inconvenience others."

The universe has a harsh way of dealing with us until we get the message: We have to keep our agreements no matter how we feel.

Body Metaphors.   A very popular way of dealing with upper limits is to take it out on our bodies. It is very common, for example, to get sick or have an accident just after a period of closeness. When you get close you go slightly out of control. This is productive, because most things that are fun and creative involve going out of control. If you are not aware of this process, you may get afraid and need to be brought back to earth sharply. Then you will bump into things, slip and fall, cut your finger, or do some other little thing that will reassert your awareness of body boundaries. Here are several real-life examples:

- A man bumped his head on his trunk lid (enough to deliver a concussion) just as the eagerly awaited birth of his first child was imminent.

75

- A woman had recently begun to nurture herself by setting up a special meditation room for herself downstairs. She went through a lot of guilt for taking time to herself, as well as guilt for using the room for such a "frivolous" purpose. She slipped and fell several times on her way down to the room. Oddly enough, she had never slipped on those stairs before.

A very useful practice with accidents and illnesses is to notice and explore your experience just prior to the incident. What were you thinking and feeling just before you cut your finger? What was going on in your relationship just before you came down with a cold? Questions like these have rewarded many people with life-changing insights into their limiting patterns.

The Positive Alternative: Creating New Channels for Positive Energy

Now that we have had a look at some of the ways human beings limit and stop the flow of positive energy in relationships, let's explore what we might do instead. The question we need to answer is: How can we rise higher and higher without bringing ourselves down?

Talk About It

It is important to learn how to communicate freely about the upper-limits problem. In an enlightening relationship, both people must work on the skills of speaking the truth about what is going on inside them. Here are some examples of how to communicate about upper limits:

- "Last night we got so close that today I feel myself wanting to pull back. I'm scared of being loved this much."
- "I've been having a lot of worry thoughts about your leaving me. Since I know intellectually that you aren't, and since I've never felt closer to you, I think I must be going through some fears of getting close."
- "When you give me so much love, sometimes I feel like running away. I don't feel that I deserve it."
- "I think I stubbed my toe yesterday to bring myself down because I was scared to feel as good as I've felt with you lately."

76

- "I feel like I'm about to start an argument with you. I'm noticing lots of little things that irritate me. I wonder if it's because I'm hitting my limit of being able to handle all the love I've been getting from you?"

We found that it took many months of practice in our own relationship to learn how to communicate clearly as we were going through our upper limits. There is always an incredibly strong pull to blame and find fault, to take seriously the grit that is coming up in the mind and body. With practice, though, we found that it became possible to spot upper-limits problems as they were emerging so we could talk about them and transcend them very quickly. Here is a recent example of one upper-limits incident of ours, recalled by Kathlyn.

> I had a disturbing dream that Gay was angry at me. Instead of brooding about it or trying to forget it, which would have been old patterns of mine, I described the dream to Gay. He could have not listened, gotten defensive, gotten mad, or tried to interpret my experience. Instead he listened, then asked me what part of myself each part of the dream represented. As a result, it became clear that I was tuning in to a deep level of his old anger at women. My issue was feeling small around men's anger. After talking, we felt very close.

Make Room to Grow

A key agreement in an enlightening relationship is that it is all right for both people to take space and time for themselves. This process allows people to integrate the positive energy they have received from the other person. There are times when the only way to deal with what is emerging is to go off on your own for an hour or a week. If taking space is agreed upon as a necessary and permissible part of the relationship, it often does not require long periods of time for the needed integration to occur. Many people, though, have difficulty with giving themselves and their partners permission to take space. Some of the specific fears that come up are:

- "If I let her or him go, I'm afraid she or he won't love me when he or she comes back."
- "If I take space myself, I'm afraid they won't love me when I get back."
- "I'm afraid of letting go of control over you."
- "I'm afraid of being alone."

For people in entanglements, taking space brings up fear of losing. People in enlightening relationships take space because they are committed to the growth of the relationship. They realize that for the relationship to be nurtured, they must take time and space to discharge grit, get established at a new, higher level of energy, or reaffirm their individual connection to the universe.

It takes courage to care enough about yourself and your relationship to take time off. In an enlightening relationship, it is essential for both people to be willing to give space and take it for themselves. With freedom to be separate, greater closeness can occur.

Touch and Movement

When you go beyond the upper limit of the amount of love and positive energy you have been used to handling, you expand your boundaries. Imagine that you have been wearing a tight corset for a long time. Then someone comes along, unzips you, and invites you to breathe fully and deeply. You would probably feel great, but you would probably feel strange until you got familiar with the greater amount of space and freedom you had. Love works like that. When you receive and give love, your boundaries expand. You then need to become established and comfortable at the new expanded level. Touch and movement are two excellent ways of becoming comfortable with bigger boundaries. If we don't take care to explore the new boundaries consciously, we will often find ways of doing it unconsciously.

Having your partner give you a massage is a superb way of using touch to give you a sense of your new boundaries. Massage, of course, has other benefits (for example, it feels good). Movement, like dancing, running, aerobics, and walking, are also splendid ways of getting your feet on the ground after an excursion into the higher reaches of love and positive energy.

Make Positive Agreements
with the Universe

Often our fundamental agreements with the universe are made when we are young and under stress. Later, these agreements limit us. Here are some examples of limiting agreements that people have had to sort through later:

- "Since this is such a crazy world, I'm not going to play."
- "If I stop feeling and seeing what's going on around me, maybe I won't hurt so much."
- "If you won't hurt me anymore, I'll agree to be invisible."

Once we escape the powerless state of childhood, it is up to us to strike a better bargain with the universe. It is possible to be conscious about the agreements you make, setting the stage for an entirely different life experience to unfold. One such agreement is that you are willing to establish yourself at higher and higher levels of positive energy without inconveniencing yourself or anyone else. This agreement can prevent many arguments and stubbed toes. Often we set up a sharp encounter with other people or the universe just after rising to a higher level of positive energy. The purpose of the encounter is to get us grounded and established at the new level. However, doing it that way creates wear and tear on ourselves and other people. If you like, you can take total responsibility for establishing yourself at the higher level with positive consequences all around. As an experiment, try on the following statement: I'm willing to establish myself at higher and higher levels of positive energy with totally positive consequences for me and others. Having a highly evolved intention like this one can prevent many unpleasant encounters with the world around you.

Another basic agreement you can make with the universe is that you are willing to learn your lessons in ways that are kindly to yourself and others. Life is full of lessons. If we think our lessons have to be hard, then that's what we will tend to get.

Many people have found that they can clear a path for themselves through the world by changing their basic beliefs. As an experiment, try on the following intention: I am willing to learn my lessons in ways that are kindly to me and everyone else.

Nobody needs to have a relentlessly hard time of it, and deep inside none of us really wants to. We think we have to learn by hard knocks because that is what we have been taught. Let's try it a different way, though, to find out if we like it better.

After a certain point in evolution, it is necessary to use your body to flesh out your higher intentions. We can go only so far with our minds, magnificent though they are. As our intentions become higher we have to learn to ride waves of positive energy inside ourselves. As positive energy polishes our inner body, we have to cooperate with it by finding ways to nurture and support its flow. We have found dance and other movement activities like aerobics to be essential in letting more energy through. We have also found ourselves paying a great deal more attention to diet and nutrition, discovering which foods elevate us and which ones bring us down. Ultimately, the play of positive energy in the body becomes a fascinating game of its own, a journey to find how the dance with each other and with the universe can be made increasingly more vibrant.

It takes courage to open yourself to higher levels of positive energy. To do so is to break through the limits of the past and move into unexplored terrain. Many people prefer to nap through life, waking occasionally to eat or express an opinion. If you are reading this book, though, you have already awakened, and now your tasks are becoming clearer.

You begin by spotting ways you limit your positive energy by projecting, being a victim, not feeling, telling lies, and breaking agreements. Then you open up new channels for positive energy by:

- Feeling your feelings
- Telling the truth
- Keeping your agreements
- Taking space
- Touching and being touched
- Moving
- Making growthful agreements with the universe

All of these tools allow you to experience a clearer flow of positive energy between your core and the world around you. Life becomes a process of rising to higher and higher levels of giving and receiving positive energy.

ten
Specific
Problem-Solving
Strategies

In this chapter we will explore specific ways of solving problems when they emerge. These strategies are based on approaches that have worked with both individuals and couples in the authors' experiences in therapy and workshops over the last ten years.

The first major problem in solving problems is getting both people interested in them. Often in relationships, one person is more interested in solving problems than the other person. So, the first thing to ask ourselves is: Am I actually interested in the growth of this relationship? When two people in a relationship can agree that they are committed to solving their problems, some vibrant possibilities open up.

Formidable hurdles must be leaped to arrive at this commitment. Many people, remember, are in relationships for reasons other than enlightenment. It may be more important, for example, to perpetuate some personality pattern from the past. For them, it is more important to grind an old axe than it is to have a growing relationship. Too, many people are interested not in solving problems but in justifying some already arrived-at decision.

What does it look like when one or both people in a relationship are not truly committed to growth? There are certain styles or patterns that are common in these sorts of relationships. Perhaps with an awareness of these styles we can trade them in for something that works better.

Escalation

It begins with a remark that sounds quite innocent:

- "Who was that on the phone?"
- "You've sure been working late a lot recently."
- "Did those pants shrink? They seem to be fitting really tight lately."

Partners trade shots with increasing intensity until a shouting match results. When the energy is spent, either the real issues emerge or, more likely, they stay submerged. Because these angry escalations resemble a sexual experience, with rising intensity and a climax, the authors call this the "Wargasm pattern."

Withdrawal

Under the stress of conflict, some people withdraw into themselves and take themselves out of contact with other people. This pattern is at the other end of the spectrum from the Wargasm.

One form of withdrawal is to back away from interactions, perhaps to sulk and not participate. Another form is to withdraw awareness so that you do not see a problem. Sometimes a mixture of the two occurs. For example, one man had the tendency to withdraw into himself when problems arose, and also to withdraw his awareness so that he did not pay attention to what was going on around him. His wife began an affair with a man who lived in part of their house. She even tried to tell her husband several times, but he refused to listen. He began taking long business trips so that he would not have to deal with what was happening at home.

For many of us it does not come easy to participate in solving problems. In painful situations, it often seems easier to retreat inside and withdraw our sensory apparatus from the world. This pattern, however, only seems to make matters worse in the long run.

Affront and Apology

A third style that does not seem to lead to enlightening relationships is that in which problems are resolved through apologies and promises to do better. There is, of course, nothing wrong with apologies and promises if they are effective. In the experience of the authors', this style is rarely effective in clearing up major issues in a relationship. Apologies do not often get to the deeper levels of what is going on.

To illustrate this style, we offer the example of a man who repeatedly broke agreements with his wife. Each time there was a furious battle which would eventually end with a demand for an apology and a promise never to do it again. It was at best a temporary solution, for the pattern would happen again a week or two later. Interestingly, he never felt good about apologizing. He did it, but something about it did not resonate with him. Yet he had no idea why he kept breaking the agreements. After much work on himself, he discovered that the pattern went back to the way he interacted with his mother. At about this time his wife realized what her end of the deal was. She had grown up in a family in which her father repeatedly broke agreements with her mother, resulting in furious brawls followed by apologies. The pattern had not worked for her parents—they divorced in their midfifties —but that did not stop the daughter from adopting the same pattern for her marriage. The story does not have a conventionally happy ending. Ultimately, she would not take responsibility for the problem at the deeper levels. She continued to demand apologies, and he became increasingly reluctant to give them once he had caught on to what the game was about. The relationship finally broke up, as is often the case when one person is willing to own responsibility and the other is not.

When affronts occur repeatedly, it is most efficient to ask ourselves: What am I doing to create these situations? In what way, and for what reasons, am I setting up my life so these things happen? In other words, if people keep stepping on my toes, it may be a waste of energy to experience each one as affront and to demand an apology. It may be smoother to find out why I am putting my toes so vulnerably in harm's way.

To take responsibility for what happens, to inquire into patterns that do not seem to be working well, are clear signs that you are ready for enlightening relationships. It signifies that you are tired of the one-up—one-down style of problem-solving in which one person has to be wrong and another right. It says that you are ready for equality. When you regard yourself as equal with all other beings, themselves equal too, then you are poised on the threshold of real magic. At this point you should not be surprised when miracles start happening to you on a regular basis.

The Miraculous Alternative

The key to handling problems in enlightening relationships is to dissolve them rather than solve them. A problem dissolves when it is experienced deeply and expressed completely. This process is not easy to master. The reward, however, is well worth the energy invested.

In order to dissolve problems, all parties must be willing to take 100 percent responsibility for creating the problem. Anything less and you have a power struggle. In a couple relationship, for example, if one person takes responsibility and the other does not, inequality exists. Enlightening relationships only occur among equals.

When a problem occurs, the first task is to get all parties to treat it as their own. If this agreement cannot be attained, keep exploring the situation until all parties can embrace this fundamental issue. Unfortunately, many relationships founder at this point.

Experiencing the Problem

Now that you have taken responsibility for the problem, how do you dissolve it? First, by experiencing it as fully as you can. To experience it means to go beneath the level of thought to see, taste, feel, and touch the problem. For example, a man who had a problem of lying to his partner tuned in to where he experienced the problem in his body. He discovered a tight ball in his stomach. When he breathed in to the spot he suddenly was flooded with tears, remembering all the times he had been punished for telling the truth as a child. The problem with his wife was simply an extension of the tight ball of fear he had carried around most of his life. When he experienced and released the fear, he had no trouble telling the truth to his wife.

Experiencing a problem means being willing to open up to it, explore it, dance with it, dream it, sleep it. The willingness to experience it seems to be the most important shift. We all have our individual ways of experiencing things, so it is not possible to say how it should be done in every case. By being willing to experience problems you automatically open up creative ways to do it. Some questions that are often helpful in experiencing problems are:

- "Where do I experience this problem in my body?"
- "What does this remind me of from the past?"
- "Am I scared? Of what?"

- "Am I angry? About what?"
- "Am I sad? About what?"
- "What do I need to communicate? To whom?"
- "Is there something or someone I am trying to control?"
- "Am I seeking approval? From whom?"
- "What do I need to love here?"

We have witnessed many seemingly miraculous changes occur when people have become willing to ask these kinds of questions. Often the biggest breakthroughs occur when a question is asked when you are feeling completely stuck. Sometimes, in fact, the act of asking the question dissolves the problem regardless of what kind of answer you get.

Enlightening Communication

Step One of enlightening problem-solving is determining if all parties are willing to take full responsibility for the problem. Step Two is experiencing the problem. Step Three is communicating about the problem in an enlightening way. To do this we have to learn a new language, one that reaches beneath blame and judgment to tell the truth of our experience.

There is one type of communication that comes from the layer of ourselves that is defensive, blaming, and judgmental. Another type comes from the deeper level of us. Here are contrasting examples of what the two levels sound like:

BLAME LEVEL	TRUTH LEVEL
"You are a bastard."	"I am hurt."
"You don't love me."	"I am feeling unlovable."
"You're gonna leave me; I just know it."	"I've got a knot in my stomach, just like the one I had when Dad left Mom."
"You don't care about me."	"You were fifteen minutes late coming home."

Sometimes the blame level contains a germ of truth. However, the full reality does not emerge until the truth level is reached.

Learning to know the truth about ourselves and communicate clearly are among the trickiest things to master in life. There are no courses in school that teach these skills; often, too, we get punished for knowing and speaking the truth. So we need to give ourselves permission to be beginners in developing these skills.

Two Examples

Here are two examples of solving problems in the way we have described. The first comes from an experience of one of the authors (KH).

> I broke a crystal wineglass in the kitchen one day. Since I had broken something else earlier in the day, I asked myself if there was some significance to those accidents that I was overlooking. Very quickly I realized the crystal was a remnant from a past relationship. The next day Gay stepped on a piece of crystal and cut his foot badly. Even though I had vacuumed the floor carefully, I had missed this piece. I asked myself if his accident involved me. I felt sadness that Gay had cut himself. When that cleared I felt some anger down in my belly. I spent some time with that, getting willing to complete any anger from that past relationship without letting it spill over onto Gay. I also got rid of the rest of the crystal, lovely though it was, so I would not continue the pattern of breaking a glass or two a year.

The next example illustrates how far we sometimes have to take problems before we turn to face them.

A former client moved away to another state. She called two weeks later to say she felt awful, had not been sleeping, and felt numb. As we talked I (KH) encouraged her to take a few deep breaths and experience what she was feeling in her body. Immediately she got in touch with what was going on. She was feeling pain about her former boyfriend, but had tried to pretend that it didn't bother her. She said she suspected that she had left town rather than look at the pain in the relationship. Although she was a thousand miles away from him, the pain had caught up with her. I encouraged her to feel the pain and to love it as much as she could. After a bit she said it was still there, but that there was "air around it." She called a few days later to say that she felt better and was ready to face forward toward her new life. She has since found challenging work and begun some new relationships.

Someone once compared enlightening problem-solving to fluffing a pillow. Instead of blaming the lumps, you simply fluff them. Fluffing means feeling a problem, talking about it at deeper and deeper levels, exploring it nonjudgmentally until it dissolves. There is no single solution to fluffing a pillow or a problem. You just keep fluffing until something more comfortable emerges. In enlightening relationships, problems are not solved but dissolved, surrounding them with more and more light until they become de-light.

eleven
Sex and Money
in Enlightening
Relationships

Sex and money are two fundamental areas in which relationships often founder. Yet troubles in these two areas can provide the fuel for many enlightening moments. Sex and money are so complicated that a separate book could be written about how to handle these two areas in enlightening relationships. At the same time, the problems and their solutions are quite simple when viewed in the correct way. In this chapter we will discuss a few of the major issues and describe what we, the authors, have found to be workable and enlightening solutions.

SEX

To begin, here is a catalogue of some of the troubles with sex that people have discussed in therapy and in the authors' workshops:

1. I want sex more often than my partner does.
2. I want sex less often than my partner does.
3. Often I just want to be held and not make love.

4. I use sex to meet other needs [for example, to exert power or control].

5. I withhold sex to punish my partner.

6. I have trouble talking about sex (for example, it's hard to ask for what I want).

7. I can't seem to have love and sex at the same time.

8. My partner doesn't consider my pleasure, only his or hers.

9. I feel guilty about sexual pleasure.

10. I'm afraid to feel my sexual feelings intensely.

Problems like these are very common. In the Western world, where everything from blue jeans to bifocals are sold with sex, it is extremely difficult to know how we actually feel about our sexuality. Too, we are only eighty years or so away from a time when a heady rush could be induced by the glimpse of a naked ankle. It is no wonder we have our troubles with exploring and talking about our sexuality.

At the root of our sexual issues are two fears: the fear of opening up to sexuality and the fear of expressing it, which includes talking about it. We can readily see where these fears come from. In growing up, few of us receive much information on our awakening sexuality. One woman remembers that the entirety of sex information she received from her family came on her wedding day in 1960. Her very religious mother reeled into the room, grabbed her by the shoulders, and screamed, "Don't forget, withdrawal is a mortal sin." That was it. She didn't even know what withdrawal was. Sometimes, there is even less said about sex. In addition, our sexual feelings themselves are often confusing to us. One day we are striding along through childhood, when a switch is suddenly flipped and we become sexual. No matter whether these feelings come on gently or like a torrent, they are still the subject of much confusion to us. We fear opening up to these mysterious feelings. Where will they take us? Will we get into trouble there?

The fear of expressing our sexuality is complicated also. If we aren't smart about expressing our sexuality, all sorts of troubles can ensue, from simple emotional turmoil to accidental pregnancy. In addition, children are sometimes punished for even mentioning the subject of sex. One of the authors (GH) recalls growing up in the mid-1950s in a family where sex was a taboo subject. He brought the subject up only two times, and it created such an uproar with his mother (anger, fits of

94

sobbing, sullen withdrawal) that he quickly learned not to introduce that subject again. It wasn't until much later in life that he became comfortable with talking about sex.

To clear up sexual problems and make the most of the gift of sexuality, it is useful to express the following intention: I'm willing to be open to my full sexuality and to express it in ways that support my evolution totally. At the core of us is a deep knowledge that our sexuality is just fine. All we have to learn to do is express it clearly, in ways that yield positive consequences for us and others.

The two finest aphrodisiacs the authors have discovered are emotional honesty and clear communication. Knowing how you feel and what you want, and being willing to say these things clearly to people you care about, can be the launch pad for many high sexual experiences. Emotional honesty lines you up with your own core feelings, and clear communication puts you straight with the world around you. Here are some examples of emotional honesty and clear communication that have turned people on in enlightening relationships. Some of these may sound trivial, but they are not. In the case of the first one, for example, the person had withheld it for years although she had felt it. When it was expressed, she felt turned on and she got what she wanted.

- "I would like you to touch and hold me more before we make love."
- "I feel sexual feelings for other people sometimes."
- "I want you to touch my clitoris *very gently*."
- "I would like you to be on top of me more often."
- "Touch me here just as I come."
- "I want you just to hold me for a while."
- "I love it when you whisper to me while we are making love."

It is not an easy thing to be honest with ourselves about our deepest feelings and to express them to each other. Both acts are like a miracle pill you have to swallow on faith. Perhaps all of us are afraid that if we are honest everything will fall apart. Sometimes it does. And yet, in our experience in working with thousands of people over the last decade, we have not seen a single incident where honesty and clear communication did not ultimately bring about healing and greater happiness to those concerned.

High Fidelity

What of sexual feelings for others outside your primary relationship? What of fidelity, infidelity, jealousy? These are highly charged issues, not easily solved by conventional thinking. However, when we look at them in a fresh way they really are not so complicated.

It is natural to experience sexual feelings for people other than your primary partner. So we have to make sure we give ourselves permission to experience these feelings. If sexual feelings are resisted or denied, they can become a very big deal. Often, if we simply go ahead and let ourselves feel sexy toward other people, the feeling doesn't last very long.

If you are going to act on those feelings and have outside sexual experiences, be prepared to step into a three-ring circus. If you do not communicate to your partner what you are doing, a deep vibration is set up in the relationship that will have to emerge and be resolved at some time. If you choose to tell the truth of what you are doing, the activity in the circus can get intense very quickly. Few of us handle the naked truth without strong reaction. After seeing people do it both ways (lie versus tell the truth) a few hundred times, we have come to feel even more strongly that telling the truth works better. Lying is definitely no fun, and even if you are lying to protect someone (you, your partner, the children, the relationship), lying almost always ends up hurting them more.

If the flow of clear communication is kept alive in a relationship by sharing even such feelings as sexual attraction to other people, the relationship can grow very quickly. This is because the increased energy from the sexual feelings is being kept within the relationship. If suppression or denial occurs, energy is taken out of the relationship; the result is flatness and distortion.

We have discovered in our own relationship that when we are honest with ourselves and communicate clearly, we want to be sexual only with each other. Sexual feelings for other people may come up from time to time, but they are not a big deal. We have found the same phenomenon with a number of other people with whom we have worked. When the intentions are clear and the channels of positive energy and communication are open, fidelity naturally occurs. This is what we mean by the term "High Fidelity."

Much of what passes for fidelity between partners is based on fear of denial. I'm afraid of getting caught, so I don't mess around. Or I suppress my sexual interest in other people and pretend that it doesn't exist.

High Fidelity is not based on fear or denial. It is based on clear intentions and open communication; it thrives on the aphrodisiacal qualities of knowing and telling the truth.

MONEY

As with sex, money issues often trip up people who have the highest intentions in relationship. There are two main problems to watch out for in regard to money. The first is that money is often a symbol of underlying inequality and power struggles in the relationship. The second is that money and material things can be used as a substitute for love and/or clear communication.

When there are undercurrents of power struggle and inequality going on in a relationship, they are almost inevitably expressed through the symbol of money struggles. Money is tangible, and most people hold the belief that there is not enough of it to go around. So it is a perfect screen on which to project any deeper issues in the relationship. The reality of how much money is available does not seem to be a major factor in many money struggles. For example, in one relationship where the reality is that they are in the millionaire bracket, the woman still has to ask her husband for weekly grocery money and the request frequently triggers an argument. Here the issue clearly is not about money but about keeping the woman in a powerless and subservient position. When money struggles are in the air, then, we first need to ask ourselves questions like:

- Is someone trying to exert control through money?
- Is anyone being made to feel powerless through the control of money?
- Do we feel equal in regard to money?

Resolving money struggles is particularly tricky when there is in fact an unequal status in the relationship. For example, one couple has been married nearly forty years, but since the woman has never worked, she has never overcome the feeling that she is always spending HIS money.

Therefore, even though they have plenty of money, she finds it very difficult to spend any on herself. Since society contains at present many such inequalities, there are going to have to be many courageous assertions and negotiations among men and women before the problem is straightened out.

Another common problem in relationships is that money and material objects can become substitutes for love, commitment, and clear communication. Naturally, advertising and marketing have a strong vested interest in having us buy jewelry and perfume to express love and commitment, to purchase roses to buy forgiveness, to buy a sheer nightgown to make up for an argument, and so on. In therapy, we have worked with couples who had spent hundreds of thousands of dollars on diamonds and material things in an attempt to "save" or revive the relationship. These material things were attempts to bury some deeper distortion or problem that had occurred in the relationship. There is, of course, nothing wrong with material objects, but when they are substitutes for something that needs to be clearly said, the problem will still be there when the excitement of the bauble has worn off. We want to avoid the trap symbolized by the woman who said, "I can always tell when my husband ends one of his affairs because he buys *me* a piece of jewelry."

Money and sex are sensitive areas that can be of concern to those in enlightening relationships. We have discussed some of the most common issues; there are thousands of permutations of the main issues that are specific to each relationship. For those people who are courageous enough to set clear intentions and communicate what is in their hearts with integrity, even these troublesome areas can bring enlightenment.

twelve
Experiments in Enlightening Relationships

This chapter contains movement experiments and communication activities that illustrate the major principles and issues discussed in this book. In order to enlighten a relationship, it is essential to experience the concepts as well as to understand them intellectually.

Each activity has an introduction that explains its purpose. The instructions are designed to be read and followed directly from the book. Choose a comfortable time and place to explore these activities. You can choose between long experiments or short, those that are playful or those that are more deeply revealing. Feel free to expand and adapt these structures to your relationship and your needs. We have had a great deal of enlightening fun with these activities and hope you will too.

PARTNER STRETCHING

In this activity you can support your partner's expansion and growth. You can also learn new ways to directly support each other.

Directions

Face each other and stand with your legs about hip-width apart. Hold your partner's wrists firmly with your hands in the same way that trapeze artists do. Begin very gently and slowly to lean back from each other and feel where that stretches you. Then come back to supporting your own weight. Lean away again in a different direction, keeping your knees soft. Then come back to center.

Now experiment for several minutes using each other's weight to stretch your own body. You can turn your body and stand more on one leg to reach different areas, such as your sides. Then return to standing supporting your own weight, gently release wrists, and shake out your body.

BEING CLOSE—GETTING SEPARATE

One of the major dynamic issues in relationships is how comfortable we are with the cycle of getting close to another person and seeking individual space. This activity will give you a framework in which to explore body cues and nonverbal communication with your partner that may show you your preferences and your blind spots in the space dance of relationship. This activity explores the fundamental pulsation in relationships — getting close and getting separate. If you have time to do only one activity in this section, we recommend that this be the one. You can do this experiment in pairs or in larger groups. You will have more movement possibilities in an open space.

Directions

Begin by paying close attention to yourself as you move about the room. Each of you should keep moving as fast or slowly as you wish, noticing that your preference may change. Let yourself move as close to your partner as you wish, then begin moving away as far as you want to before you start coming close again. Continue this spacial yo-yo for a few minutes. Observe how you see your partner, any internal tugs or pressures as you move closer or further away, and your connection with yourself.

Now take a few minutes to share your experience with your partner. Stick to "I" statements; for example, "I felt a tightening in my chest when you turned away." Let each of you have time to speak and to listen. Give yourself permission to be surprised.

The next part of this activity has a mover and a responder. Decide who will take which part first. Now, responder, you are going to stand in one spot and use your hands to signal the mover. Mover, you are going to resume moving closer to and further away from the responder. When the mover is as close as you want, responder, raise your hands, and at that signal, mover, you will start walking further away. When the mover is as far away as you wish at that moment, responder, raise your hands again to signal the mover to come closer again.

The mover will keep moving without pausing. Start very slowly so you will have an opportunity to sense all the levels of response in yourself. After a few minutes, mover, experiment with different speeds, levels in space, and directions that you move.

Take five or ten minutes for this part. At the end of this time exchange roles and begin again very slowly. Recognize that each pulsation of closer and further away may be different.

When each of you has experimented with both roles, take some time to talk about your experience and your discoveries. You may have uncovered some patterns you had not noticed before. You may have a request for your partner or something you realize you need to explore further. Risk taking the attitude that this activity was an unopened treasure chest full of jewels that will enhance your relating. Note down any agreements you make. Then take a moment to nonverbally acknowledge your partner.

POWER POLARITIES

Power struggles have to have opposites. If there is a winner, there must be a loser. In relationships that are based on the win-lose belief, scarcity is the force that drives us to outmaneuver our partner. There is only so much space, love, or freedom, and we need to get ours! This activity will give you the opportunity to take a reading of your current investment in power struggles with your partner. The structures are very simple, so experiment with any variations that occur to you.

Directions

Begin by facing each other, and move in the following way: when one of you comes forward, the other must back up. Conversely, if one of you retreats, the other must move forward. Keep moving without stopping for a few minutes.

Now change the structure to the vertical dimension. If one of you is high in space, the other must go low to the same degree. If you lie on the floor, for example, your partner should stretch up to the ceiling.

As in the last part, keep moving for a few minutes.

This polarity is about how much psychic space you allow yourself and your partner. If one of you is feeling GREAT, does the other become depressed or try to depress the first one? If one of you feels low energy, does that pull on the other or create a sense of guilt in either of you? The previous experiments gave you some information about how attached you are to your partner moving about in the world. Spend a few minutes now talking about anything you discovered.

Now we will extend these activities a little by playing follow-the-leader. One of you be in charge first, and play with leading your partner around the room with different contact points: hold their hand, push their shoulders, drape an arm around their shoulders, grip an elbow, hold an ear. Create as many contact spots as you can imagine. Follower, at first be very cooperative. Just go anywhere they lead you as fast or slow as they wish. After a few minutes let yourself get in touch with the part of you that DOESN'T WANT TO GO. Start resisting with the intention of discovering how you react to pressure. Just a minute or so of this part seems sufficient. Don't be surprised if you feel tired; resistance takes lots of energy.

Now switch roles; follower become leader. Begin by experimenting with many points of contact and lots of cooperation. Allow this time to be different, to develop in its own direction. After a few minutes, follower, it is your turn to resist. Open up to explore your style of not wanting to go. Some people go rigid, others collapse, some squirm and wiggle away, others go on the offensive. What is your individual style?

When we become aware of our internal preferences we can recognize them before they start taking over in patterns that become power struggles. Take time to share your experiences in these activities.

EXPLORING INTENTIONS

Intentions are like the foundation for a building. They determine what can be built, how high it can go, and how strong the structure of your relationships can be. Whatever we communicate to our partner reflects our intention. Our ability to solve problems is especially sensitive to underlying intentions. This activity can be used to explore different intentions and their impact on the quality of your relating. You may decide to focus on one of the following intentions or explore the whole series.

Directions

Face your partner, either sitting or standing, and choose a leader. Follower, you are going to move exactly as the leader does, as if you were looking in a mirror. Leader, begin moving slowly to allow the follower time to match your unique style. When you feel yourselves moving together, the leader will begin to explore different intentions. You won't need to do anything differently; just actively think the intention as you move. Exchange roles after each intention, so you will remain parallel in your exploration.

- Start with the intention to do it perfectly. Intend to mirror your partner with no mistakes, to do it just right. Continue with this intention for a few minutes, noticing how you feel in your body and how you experience your partner.

- Mirror now with the intention of getting your partner's approval. Let your movement flow out of the intention to get a seal of approval that only your partner can supply.

- Let your intention shift to being right, knowing better. See if your intention results in any subtly critical or disapproving behavior. Invite any patterns into awareness.

- Let the intention to be fully present flood your body as you move. Intend to be here with all of you.

- Both of you move with the intention of being with your partner. Loosen any holding onto doing exactly the same movement and let your intention shape your movement.

Verbally explore the effect of your different intentions on what you experienced.

OK—NOT OK

In this activity you will get a chance to clean out the closet. The debris consists of old roles and behaviors that may be spilling out into your relationship. This activity can also increase your listening and observing potential.

Directions

Take turns letting your whole body try on messages you received as a child about what behavior was OK. Some familiar messages are: stand up straight; keep your belly in; be still; look pleasant; stand tall; be graceful; etc. Repeat those familiar messages to yourself and see how your body carries them. Partner, watch and help your partner notice if those messages, that way of moving the body, is familiar. You may be behaving as if those instructions still have power and may have forgotten that you have choice about your relationship to your body. When you have both tried on several OK messages and gotten a chance to notice whether you are choosing them or doing them automatically, shake your arms and legs for a moment.

Then take turns sharing the ways your body carries not-OK messages. Some familiar not-OK messages are: don't slouch; take that sulking to your room; that's not ladylike; don't sprawl all over the place; don't be a sissy; etc. Explore your past for messages about behaviors that were not OK, and try on the forbidden action. How does that feel to your body? What does your partner notice when you let your body move in ways you learned were not all right? Take turns, and be sure to observe with love.

After exchanging body positions, you may decide that some behaviors are archaic and best changed or dropped. Talk to your partner about ways you can support each other in renewing your relationship with your body and staying in touch with your changing needs.

ENLIVENING

Nothing seems to deaden the joyful spark in relationship faster than repetition. The choice to settle for security and sameness often leads to boredom. Enlivening at all levels comes from variety, doing it differently. Experiment with this activity with the intention of changing your perspective, opening yourself to other possibilities.

Directions

Put on some music you enjoy. One partner will move any way he or she likes, on the floor stretching, sitting or standing, swinging, rolling, or just shuffling around. The other partner's task is to notice when the mover begins repeating, either in the quality of the movement or the pattern. When the noticer observes repetition, interrupt the mover. Try both verbal and nonverbal methods. Explore lots of ways of interrupting him or her, including changing your own attitudes as you observe. After several minutes switch roles. When you have both experienced moving and enlivening, share your responses to the experiment. Allow for frustration and annoyance, as well as for excitement, because we can be cranky when someone awakens us from a nap.

As a variation to this activity, you may experiment with some routine you have in your relationship and change some aspect of it. For example, if you always sleep on the same side of the bed, change sides. If you always drive the car, let your partner. If dinner is always at 6:00 P.M. sharp, try a different schedule. Looking for ways to open new pathways in our relationships supports growth and generates sparks.

PAIRED WALKING

We have used this simple activity a great deal to help partners get in touch with and share their preferred rhythms, their relationship to time and everything that follow time: decision-making, recreation and vacation choices, daily cycles of rest and activity, etc. Give yourself permission to move with your partner as if you had just met. It is especially fun to do paired walking outside.

Directions

One of you begin walking in your most familiar style. Do not try to have perfect posture or adjust for your partner; just walk along, changing direction as you desire. Partner, you are going to follow behind. Take as much time as you need to match your partner's walk exactly. Notice how they hold their head, how they swing their arms, in what direction they swivel their hips and place their feet. Let your body take on the whole body-sense of their walk. Continue for several minutes, and then exchange roles.

Once you have exchanged roles, you might try several variations:

- Walk beside your partner, and try to match his or her walk without turning your head to notice.
- Leader, try changing your speed after your partner is matching you.
- Once the follower has matched your walk, leader, move aside and let him or her continue walking as you do. What do you notice?
- When your walking matches, leader, try thinking about something that is troubling you without telling your partner. Notice if your partner comments on any changes in your walk. Try on different feelings, such as irritation, sadness, and excitement, and see if your partner notices any alteration or any change in his or her feelings.

MOVEMENT CONVERSATIONS

This activity can help you notice how comfortable you are with the male and female aspects of yourself. As you exchange movement statements with your partner, you may begin to enjoy altering and expanding your expression.

Directions

Begin sitting facing your partner. When you start this activity, take turns "speaking" with your gestures while your partner watches. Later on you may find your conversation overlapping.

Start by letting just your hands and arms speak for you. Take turns letting your hands be:

- shy
- silly
- irritated
- excited
- depressed

- strong and forceful
- seductive
- just the way you feel right now

Now let your hands rest while you take turns making faces at each other. Pull from your memory of being a kid, and try on the most outrageous faces you can. Add sounds.

Stand up now, and let as much of your whole body as you wish participate in movement and gesture exchanges that are:

- huge, giant-sized
- teeny-tiny
- only sharp angles and straight lines
- curved lines in space
- like moving underwater
- like feathers floating on the breeze
- zinging and flashing

Now exchange movements that express your ideas of masculinity and femininity. Feel free to exaggerate your gestures, to surprise yourself.

Save time when you finish to talk over your experiences.

BELLY DANCE

This activity explores the question: Can I be all of me and still be fully in touch with my partner? Use some lively music that you enjoy as background to this activity.

Directions

Stand belly to belly with your partner, arms outstretched, legs well balanced under you. Each of you move with the intention of taking up your full space, being as big as you are. Let your out-breath flow through your partner out into the universe. Play with touching the whole world through your partner. Continue for several minutes, then draw apart from each other and bounce up and down for a minute or so to ground yourself at this new energy level.

MOLDING

This activity is a variation of the statues game you may have played as children. It will give you a chance to explore attitudes about role behavior that we usually take for granted. Let yourself question the source of your attitudes and your assumptions.

Directions

Take turns molding each other's bodies as if they were clay you are shaping. Form your partner's body into your ideal male or female. Remember as your ideas change that clay can be remolded easily. After your partner is molded, have him or her begin to walk and make any additional suggestions to help him or her fit that mold. Give feedback about how you feel standing and moving in that role.

TAMING THE UPPER-LIMITS DRAGON

When we understand that the only problem we really have in relationship is the upper-limits problem, getting more love than we know how to handle, we can ride the upper-limits dragon more easily. We can begin to notice our unique thoughts and behavior that signal an upper-limits issue. This activity can assist you in developing the skill to stay conscious longer before an old pattern takes over. Eventually, upper-limits issues can be noticed, acknowledged, and resolved quickly and with love. You can practice this skill with a partner or alone at any time in any setting.

Directions

Review in your mind the most recent positive experience you had in your relationship. As you review let one part of your mind notice any fleeting negative thoughts. They may be disguised as worry thoughts, such as something going wrong (rain, car breaking down), something going to happen before we get there (where your mind leaves the present moment), someone going to get hurt (the plane is going to crash), etc. By reviewing positive experiences you can become aware of your most common upper limits thoughts and images.

It is important to remember that these mental images occur *before* an actual obstacle appears, such as stubbing your toe, having an argument out of the blue, missing an appointment. So another kind of review is to remember the last accident or illness you experienced and recall what was going on in your life and relationship just before the obstacle appeared. The chapter on upper limits gives many examples of this phenomenon.

With these reviews fresh in your mind, you can practice taking a thought or image and asking yourself, "How am I experiencing this in my body?" Pause after asking this question and notice any changes in your breath, pains or pressures anywhere in your body, strange sensations, tightness. Take the most noticable body phenomenon and breathe into it (even if it is in your big toe). Do not analyze or ask what to do about it, just be there. After a bit you will probably notice that the experience shifts in some way, and you may get a sudden idea of what this is about in your life. When your experience shifts, take a few deep breaths and stretch your body, especially your neck and torso. You can repeat this sequence as often as you wish, going back to thoughts, tracing them to their experience in your body, loving them, watching them dissolve.

POSITIONS

Fear of letting go is one of the big problems we face in life and in our relationships. Loss of control, fear of catastrophe, lead us to protect ourselves from the unknown by taking positions about life. Here are some common positions we have heard:

- "I have to do it right."
- "I don't have time."
- "I have to keep it together."
- "I'll show you."
- "It's not fair."

111

Positions cause difficulty because they are red lights; we perceive them as a danger signal and shut down, decrease our aliveness. Each mental position we take has a direct physical correlate. We sculpt our bodies and our possibilities by the attitudes we adopt. This experiment is designed to explore positions and their effect on our interactions and perceptions. Another aspect of this experiment is to experience directly the vitality and connection to life that blossom when we dissolve old attitudes about life.

Directions

Brainstorm with your partner for a few minutes and write down familiar thoughts and expressions, phrases you each find yourselves repeating internally or out loud. From that list choose a phrase to try on with your whole body. One partner repeat your phrase out loud several times while gesturing simultaneously. The other partner will encourage you to exaggerate your tone of voice and your movements. It is like opera; you will play to the back row with larger-than-life mannerisms. When you both feel and see that the voice and gestures match in intensity, hold that position for a minute or so. Feel its effects on your sense of yourself, the way you experience your partner, what you see around you. Notice your breath and the particular tension of this position. After a minute or two, both of you begin to actively love that position about life. Breathe into it, make space around it, love whatever created the need for that position. Allow your love to dissolve the position in whatever way feels best, be it abrupt or melting. Then switch roles and let the reflector take a position to explore.

As a variation, the reflector can mirror the partner taking the position. As you try on your partner's position with your own body, you can experience his or her attitudes more deeply. You can also add to the innovative possibilities in the dissolving phase.

SETTING INTENTIONS

This communication activity uses the intentions listed in Chapter Six in a structure that allows you to explore your communication style with each other.

Directions

Stand facing each other, with the speaker holding the book open to the list of intentions. Let one of you go through all seven intentions before you switch roles. Speaker, say each intention out loud to your partner, then pause for ten to fifteen seconds afterward to notice any thoughts, feelings, or images that arise in your mind. Listener, you have two major tasks. First, listen with your whole body as your partner says an intention. Do you have any internal responses to that intention? If so, notice and acknowledge them. Second, notice how the speaker delivers the communication. Is his or her body aligned, or does some body part list or slump? Listen to the tone of voice; watch for mannerisms or gestures that detract from the direct communication of the intention. Give the speaker feedback about what you notice.

Repeat each intention until the listener feels, "Yes, I got it, that's clear. I hear you." Let your overall intention in this activity be to communicate directly and truthfully. When one partner has completed the list, switch roles.

LIST OF INTENTIONS

- I am willing to be totally independent and totally close.
- I am willing to have my relationships be a force that takes me to full enlightenment.
- I am willing to clear up anything in the way of my full enlightenment and ability to be close.
- I am willing to have other people be fully empowered in my presence.
- I am willing to transform myself in whatever ways are necessary to serve my highest evolution and have the highest quality relationships with others.
- I am willing to take space as often as necessary to nurture myself and the relationship.
- I am willing to have our relationship be about giving and receiving maximum positive energy.

INCREASING LOVE

One of our biggest issues as humans is acknowledging our innate lovableness. Each of us has pockets of experience and feeling that we just

know are not lovable. Our relationships are hampered by this fundamental illusion, as we try to hide our unlovable places, improve them, or
make up for them. The purpose of this communication activity is to
discover that all of you is totally lovable.

Directions

Sit cross-legged facing each other (or sit in chairs), and hold hands
lightly. Continue looking at each other as you repeat this phrase silently,
"You are totally lovable." Pause after each repetition for several seconds, and notice any internal response.

Now take turns repeating this phrase out loud, again pausing
between repetitions. Then take time to share memories or issues that
may have arisen. You can add another round of exchange here in which
you say, "I am totally lovable," until you feel the truth of that phrase
deeply.

Now each of you identify a place in your body that feels unlovable. One at a time, tell your partner where you feel unlovable, and let
them actively love that part of you until you feel directly in touch with its
lovableness. The partner who is loving can let love stream from his or
her eyes and hands and do whatever seems necessary to communicate
the other partner's total lovableness. You can repeat this phrase with
other parts of you until you feel filled with love.

You might find you have lots of energy following this activity, and
you might want to find a new way to share that love with each other.

FEEDBACK

Communication has many levels. To enrich your relationship, this activity expands the routes that we generally travel in our interactions. It is
designed to increase your awareness of the subtle cues to which you
respond. When we unconsciously respond to nonverbal signals, mixed
messages, and crossed communication can begin to impede the flow of
relating.

Directions

Take turns completing the following two sentences, giving your partner
a chance to respond.

1. "I notice [a body gesture or expression], and I wonder what that means." Example: I notice that you stopped breathing just then, and I wonder what that means.

2. "I notice [a body gesture or expression], and I am afraid that it means _____." Example: I notice that your forehead is furrowed, and I am afraid it means you are angry at me.

Take time to clear up any ambiguity, to talk about what you meant to communicate, and to acknowledge any intentions you or your partner developed from this activity.

EXPRESSION CYCLES

This communication activity is designed to help you learn how you know what you want and how to express your desires clearly. We often hear, especially from women, "I don't KNOW what I want! I've never thought about it!" Learning that we are equals involves opening up to our deepest needs and wishes, noticing and dissolving whatever blocks their expression.

Directions

Part 1: Take turns completing the phrase, "Right now I feel _____." Before you say the phrase, take several deep breaths, stretch your body, and notice the tinglings, pressures, and other internal sensations. Take turns repeating this phrase several times, then use movement or a gesture to complete the sentence for several more repetitions.

Part 2: Stand facing your partner. One person will be the speaker and the other will be the listener. Speaker, repeat the phrase, "I want," as many times as you need to until you feel the phrase in your body. Listener, give your partner feedback about the tone of their voice, whether they keep eye contact, how they hold their body as they speak. Also notice your own experience. Then exchange roles.

Part 3: Take turns completing the phrase, "Right now I feel _____, and I want _____." For example, "Right now I feel irritable, and I want to take a walk." Or, "Right now I feel excited, and I want to be close to you."

COMPLETING FEELING CYCLES

This communication activity is about expanding your perception of the way energy moves in the body. It is structured to allow you and your partner to experience deep and complete feeling cycles. You may want to take two separate times to complete this activity, as it is longer and more intense than other experiments in this chapter.

Directions

One of you, the feeler, will lie down in a warm, comfortable place. Your partner, the toucher, will sit facing you at your side.

Toucher, place one hand gently on your partner's throat. Let your other hand skim over his or her torso until you click into the "anger spot." Then let your hand come to rest on that place.

Feeler, let that anger center begin to speak inside you. Let those feelings come up and begin to form in your mind. Then let the feelings turn into words; let yourself say, "I'm angry." Toucher, catch the pulsation of anger and feel it in your own body. Breathe into those feelings, and love yourself and love your partner for every ounce of anger he or she feels. When the anger subsides, toucher, tell your partner, "I love you for everything."

Now, toucher, allow the hand that was on the anger center to begin a float above your partner's torso again until you find the fear spot. Let your touch invite your partner's deepest fear right up to the top. See if you can also let that fear through your own body. Feeler, allow the fear to rise in your body until the words form, "I'm afraid." Toucher, catch each wave of fear and give it back to your partner with love. After the fear feels complete, toucher, focus on loving your partner deeply, loving your way through the fear until the connection between your hands feels clear.

Now, toucher, move the hand that was over the fear center around until you find and touch the place that says, "I'm glad to be alive," the place that shouts out the most liveliness and joy. Toucher, it is your job to let your partner know that there is no limit to positive feelings. Let your touch take the lid off. Feeler, find a phrase that best expresses your relationship to life and let that resonate in your being. Begin to ride that feeling up into words. Toucher, love that connection with life your partner has inside, and when the communication subsides, love your partner for BEING. Love him or her not for what he or she is going to do, but just for being him or herself.

Toucher, now place one hand on your partner's forehead and one on the pelvis. Imagine that a long, slender balloon that is filled with love runs up the core of his or her body. Let love gently ripple up and down the body between your hands.

Then gently separate hand contact, and take whatever time and touch you need to complete this communication. Make eye contact, hug, be with, talk.

UNDERTONES

This communication activity is about secrets we do not suspect we have. The exercise focuses on the quality of voice in conversation and the subtle shadings that flesh out the words we use. In relationship it is not so much what we say as how we say it. In this activity you will have a chance to explore these nuances.

Directions

Using a cassette deck to record your conversation, tell your partner something about your relationship you had previously withheld. Each of you take a turn. Then replay the entire conversation, listening for the undertones in your voices as you spoke. See if you can discern your intentions and your motivations in the tone of your conversation. Did you say what you really meant to say? Do you hear any unexpressed emotion? Were you justifying or blaming? Let your partner give you feedback about the things he or she heard as you spoke.

Then talk to each other about the same issue, with the intention of telling the deepest truth of your experience. Focus on just that, and notice how your communication emerges. After each of you has had a turn, listen to the tape again.

Epilogue

Human relationships have changed so much in our own lifetimes that it has been a dizzying challenge to keep up with it all. What we tried to do is to go back to ground zero and re-envision what relationships could be. We asked ourselves what we really wanted out of our relationship with each other. The answers were not complicated. We wanted fun, clear communication, minimum conflict, mutual creativity, and for our contact to be an ongoing source of psychological and spiritual growth. We then worked for several years to find out what was necessary to meet our goals. The work paid off, bringing us greater happiness, vitality, and creativity than we had ever dreamed possible. We then expanded the ideas into use with our therapy clients and workshop participants. Now we offer them to you through this book. Please accept them as experiments to be tried and verified for yourself. And please accept also our congratulations for choosing the awesomely rewarding challenge of transforming human relationships. We have found that there is no greater illumination than that which is available through close contact with each other.

Our best to you on that journey.

Index

Closeness *(cont.)*
    body language and feelings about, 52, 53
    desire for, 13, 24
    how to attain, 13, 16, 18–20
    resistance to, 4–7, 14–19
        arguments, 18–19
        illness, 19
        conflicting feelings, 16–19
        going numb, 14–15
        making wrong, 15
        power struggles, 16–18
        roles from old scripts, 16
Communication:
    activities related to, 114–17
    enlightening, 76–77, 87–88, 96–98
    See also Truth
Completing Feeling Cycles (activity), 116–17
Conflict:
    emotional, 16–19
    See also Arguments; Power struggles
Control, need for, 33
    body language and, 52
    money and, 97–98–*Couples' Journey, The* (Campbell), 17
Creativity, 9, 33, 37
    willingness and, 44
Criticism, intolerance of, 3
    See also Projection

Dancing, 78, 80
Deals, 31–32
    agreements vs., 37
Diet, 80

Ego, 13, 44
Emotions, *see* Feelings; *and specific emotions*
Enlightening relationships:
    communication style of, 76–77, 87–88, 96–98
    creation of, 37–48
        helpful intentions/agreements, 37–38, 43–48
        troublesome intentions, 38–40
    definition of, 37
    emergence into, 29–30
    entanglements vs., 29, 34
        See also Entanglements
    money issues in, 97–98
    problem solving in, 86–89

religious withdrawal vs., 45
    sex issues in, 93–97
    taking and granting space in, 47, 77–78, 80
Enlivening (activity), 106–7
Energy, *see* Negative energy; Positive energy
Entanglements:
    basic characteristics of, 29–34
    internal male/female issues in, 62–63
    nonverbal expressions of, 51–57
        space issues, 54–55, 78
        time issues, 56–57
        weight/size issues, 55–56
Equality, *see* Inequality
Escalation as response to problems, 84
Exploring Intentions (activity), 105–6
Expression Cycles (activity), 115

Fantasy as escape from closeness, 15
Fear:
    from the past, 17–18
    partner's expression of, 33
    of telling truth, 86
    See also Closeness—resistance to
Feedback (activity), 114–15
Feelings:
    cutting off, as upper-limits response, 72, 80
    partner's expression of, 32–33
    projection of, 61–65
    "special," 74
    See also specific feelings
Female issues, internal, 62–63, 108–9
Fidelity, sexual, 96–97

Homosexuality, 38–39

Illness:
    as resistance to closeness, 19
    as upper-limits response, 70, 75–76
Incompleteness as basis of entanglements, 29, 31–32, 34, 38
Increasing Love (activity), 113–14
Independence, *see* Separateness
Inequality:
    as basis of entanglements, 29, 32, 34, 86
    money issues, and, 97–98
"I-ness," 13
    See also Ego
Infidelity, 96–97

122